The Great

SONG
CYCLE

PORTLAND TO LOS ANGELES
ON TWO WHEELS AND A SONG

JOANNA WALLFISCH

UWA PUBLISHING

First published in 2019 by
UWA Publishing
Crawley, Western Australia 6009
www.uwap.uwa.edu.au

UWAP is an imprint of UWA Publishing,
a division of The University of Western Australia.

 A catalogue record for this
book is available from the
National Library of Australia

Design by Ten Deer Sigh
Printed by McPherson's Printing Group

 uwapublishing

For Alma, Manny and Lola.
May the winds always be at your backs.

CONTENTS

I'm going on a road trip,
Winding down a well worn path,
I change my background story
Every time somebody asks,
I have worn so many masks.

'Road Trip'

WE END SO WE CAN BEGIN

I wake without an alarm, my body clock now keenly tuned in to the dawn. Tightly curled up in a blue and green tartan wool blanket, lying on a thin sofa-bed mattress, I gaze into the half-light, fully rested, yet heavy with the knowledge that today is my last day on the road. My panniers lie packed at the end of the mattress, my cycling clothes neatly folded on top. I had planned to have an early start and take my time getting to Los Angeles, eek out every detail of the kilometres ahead of me, but now I lie in perfect stillness, my arms cinched against my sides like a caterpillar in stasis. The time-stopping bliss of sleep has been shattered by the dawn, and by my awareness that the inevitable finish line is but a matter of time away.

A month ago, I had envisioned this day as one of relief and excitement, ignited by joyful impatience to put down my bike and strip my behind of padded lycra once and for all. I never anticipated the whirlpool of doubt and sadness in which I am swirling now. Heat stings the back of my eyes, and a tear glides down each cheek as I stare unblinkingly at the ceiling.

Through dilated pupils I sink back into my memory, and watch as the faces and places I have encountered over the last five weeks drift before my mind's eye like distant clouds. I smile in my reverie and, as if they weren't my own, my arms find their way out of the blankets, which I throw to the side of the sofa-bed, revealing my deeply tanned legs. Limb by limb, I bring myself up to sitting.

Silence surrounds me, but for a thin, salty breeze that whispers in through the window behind the sofa. Planting my feet firmly on the worn rug, I stand and let out a sigh, wiping the tears from my face. 'Shit, Jo. How did this day already arrive?'

The painting of a wild ocean, frozen in its frame, seems to answer me: *Time plus motion, time plus motion.*

I pull on my lycra shorts and sports bra. I had saved a clean set of clothes in the bottom of my bag for this day – a special uniform for the final sprint. Half-dressed and hungry, I pad from room to room, re-examining the strange sculptures that decorate the floor, now so different in the dawn light. I look in a small mirror as I distractedly brush my teeth, my mind dwelling on what lies ahead. This evening I will be in Los Angeles.

As I roam from the bathroom to the living room and into the kitchen, I notice yellow post-it notes stuck to the walls. Looking closer, I see that each is inscribed with a message, a quote, a mantra. Just above the stove, on the same tiles I admired the night before, are two post-it notes stuck together. *Were these here last night?* I wonder as I lean in to read them.

In neat handwriting I read the words: *Your mind is playing a trick on you and making you think that something in the future is more important than this moment.*

I take the hint. It is time to get my shit together and hit the road for one last time.

MUSIC AND BLOOD

To say I was born into a musical family is like saying I was born on planet Earth. Music runs in my family like the blood that binds us. Music was as fundamental to my upbringing and existence as the food I ate. Music was everywhere, filling the very air that I breathed.

Going back just a few generations: my great-grandfather on my mother's side was the extraordinary and profoundly influential conductor Albert Coates – he conducted the London Symphony Orchestra in the rest of the program when Elgar conducted the first performance of his cello concerto. My great-grandmother on my father's side, Edith, was a violinist, and my great-grandfather Alfons Laker had a beautiful singing voice. Tragically their lives were taken by the gestapo in World War II. My paternal grandmother, Anita Wallfisch, née Lasker, is a cellist; she survived the horrors of Auschwitz-Birkenau, along with her sister Renate (their sister Marianne made her way to England earlier), because she played the cello in the women's camp orchestra, led by Alma Rosé. After the Liberation (of Belsen), she travelled to London and became a founding member of the English Chamber Orchestra. My father's father, Peter Wallfisch, was a concert pianist, born in Breslau, the same town where my grandmother was born. His survival of the Holocaust was due to his prodigious talent on the piano and thanks to a man named Emil Hauser, who was dedicated to saving young musicians and bringing them to Palestine, saving my grandfather, his brother and mother, just in time. My grandparents met again after the war by chance and a note on a scrap of paper, next to L'Opera de Paris.

My maternal grandmother, Tamara Coates, was an oboist in the English Chamber Orchestra, London Bach Orchestra and other London freelance orchestras for forty years, and also was a fine pianist and teacher. My maternal step-grandmother, Marianne Hunt, was a cellist in Melbourne, Australia. My mother, Elizabeth, née Hunt, was born in Melbourne to Tamara and Kenneth (my grandfather), who was an outstanding clarinetist in his own right, alongside his work as a professor of engineering. Two of my mother's sisters, Rosanne and Tanya, are cellists, as is my brother Simon, who is also an opera singer and specialist in Lieder. My aunt, Maya, an author and psychoanalyst, played the flute as a girl, and her son, Abraham, is a cellist. My eldest brother, Benjamin, is a conductor and major film composer. My father, Raphael, is a renowned cellist, and has recorded over seventy CDs and tours as a soloist worldwide. My mother, Elizabeth, is a celebrated baroque violinist, concert master, teacher and author, who also has a prolific discography.

The soundtrack to my childhood, from dawn until dusk, was one of scales, concertos, and partitas spilling from across the hallway and through the floorboards as my parents practised and rehearsed. My brothers and I would make our fun by turning a record of William Tell at full volume and dancing around the sitting room. If the radio was on, it would only ever be tuned to classical BBC Radio 3, or Radio 4 current affairs, and the only popular music I knew by the age of five was the Spice Girls.

My brothers and I all went through the rigmarole of private music lessons, but as the youngest child I was given more freedom from the discipline of practising, and I thoroughly rebelled against the routine, preferring to play outside, paint or improvise with song. I still managed to go through a number of instruments – violin, piano, harp and flute – but singing was the one form of musical expression I never gave up. I would sing everything, from the smallest events of my day to the songs I heard around me. At the age of eleven I was entranced by the lyrical and soaring strains of Ella Fitzgerald; at twelve I discovered the *Great American Songbook,* which I devoured and learned by heart throughout my teenage years.

It was normal that my parents should often be away on tour, not that I ever liked it much. It was hard to explain to my friends that I sometimes got homesick even when I was at home, or that neither my mum nor my dad would be picking me up from school because they were away doing concerts. Occasionally we kids lost track of whether Mum, Dad or a babysitter would pick us up, or I'd be left to go home with a friend due to a hiccup in communication. My brother Simon likes to tell the story of when the phone rang one evening and somebody asked for Elizabeth. Forgetting that Mum was away, he called out at the top of his lungs, 'Mum! Mum!' Finally the babysitter informed him, 'Simon, she's on tour in Australia.'

I missed Dad when he was away, but with his absence came the promise of his return. I was always happy when he came home, arms wide open, his cello on his back, his suit jacket crumpled from the flight – and with a suitcase full of presents. Wooden dolls from Russia, puppets from the Czech Republic, miniature perfume bottles from a market stall in Jerusalem, chocolates from Switzerland, earrings from Ireland, silk scarves from China...

When Mum went away it was a slightly different story. As soon as I got home from school I would sit by the phone and wait until she called from whichever hotel she'd arrived at and give us her contact number. This was the late 1980s and early 1990s, so we had no mobile phones or computers, and a phone call from a loved one was an event. When I was feeling especially bereft, I would call Mum, carefully spinning the numbers on the dial, starting with the fifteen-digit discount phone card number, then the country code and finally the hotel number, over and over and over again, until she picked up. If I couldn't get hold of her I would send a fax to the hotel; on one occasion, I sent a short and to the point note to the concert manager of the orchestra she was leading: 'Please send my mummy home. I need her more than you do.'

When Mum got the job as Concert Master for the Carmel Bach Festival in California I was six and was able to travel with her every summer for the next eighteen years. I would watch her from the wings as she led the orchestra, guiding her musicians in the most dignified and elegant way, and engaging with audiences as though they were her close friends. She taught me everything I know as a performer.

My parents never insisted I become a musician. They urged me to follow whichever path I wanted; if it had nothing to do with music, that would have been fine. Through my college years I tried to be other things: a painter, a chef, an acrobat. However, it was clear that music had already chosen me.

No matter how many sidesteps I took, I eventually followed my dream of becoming a jazz singer and songwriter. This ambition led me to Paris, where I busked in the streets, back to London, where I sang at Ronnie Scott's Jazz Club, and then, in 2010, to New York City, where, six years later, this story begins.

2

PROSPECT PARK

Space is but a void we gaze upon,
Throw a wish into a well and dream about a life you
want to lead, it's never easy

'When We Travel'

The idea came to me one morning after an intense swim workout at the YMCA in Park Slope, Brooklyn. The last of the grey winter slush had finally trickled from the gutters and into the drains. The once bare branches now bent and bulged with pink blossoms that decorated the sidewalks like a candy-floss carpet at the hint of a breeze. Spring in New York City was fast becoming summer.

Prospect Park was alive with picnickers, runners and early-morning dog walkers. The bandshell was being erected for the Summer Stage, promising free music and moonlit parties under the tall plane trees. The drumming circle on the south-east side of the park beat every Sunday from morning until night, and Ocean Avenue hummed with the rhythms of Africa, South America and the Caribbean.

It was 2016, and Brooklyn had been my home, my teacher and my muse since 2010. As I ploughed through the warm, chlorinated water of the 25-metre basement swimming pool, keeping pace with my training buddy, Haggai, I mentally flipped through some of the intense ups and downs of the last six years. With every stroke, followed by a twist of my face to the surface for a swift gulp of air, then another pull through the water, I was distracted by my uncertainty about what lay ahead of me. Swimming was my safe haven. As long as I was swimming, I was untouchable, strong, in control.

After a brief pause at the wall, Haggai called the last set, and I replied, doubling it. We were exhausted, having swum 2500 metres already, but I wasn't ready to face the rest of the day.

'Okay, Jo,' he said. 'This is what we will do. We sprint these last few lengths. Butterfly. No breathing until the end of the lane. Then we will forget that we are Jewish or vegetarian or whatever other bullshit excuse, and we will eat ham and cheese croissants across the road, and you will tell me what the fuck is wrong. Deal?'

I nodded, filled my lungs and flew off the end of the wall, kicking hard, opening my arms wide and high over the surface of the water, and letting the surge of adrenaline block out the anxiety I had been feeling.

My skin smelled of soap and chlorine, my braided hair was dripping, and my face was perspiring unstoppably under the Brooklyn sun. Haggai treated me to breakfast at our favourite cafe, Patisserie Colson, on 9th Street. We sat on the bench outside and balanced our coffee cups on the wonky wooden slats, our plates upon our knees.

'Jo, what's up?' Haggai asked, and took the first bite of his croissant, closing his eyes in delight.

'Ugh, I don't know,' I said. 'I just feel tangled up right now.'

'Mmm?' he replied, mouth full.

'Well, I'm about to release my new album and I honestly don't know if I can face touring it. Not one venue seems to be prepared to shell out a fee for a string quartet, and I certainly can't afford to pay for one myself. Not to mention the emotion of performing an album I recorded with my ex.' Even saying this out loud brought a lump to my throat.

'I hear you. So what are you going to do? I mean, you must tour the album, I'm sorry to say. What is your bigger purpose?' Haggai asked, his frankness accentuated by his thick Israeli accent. 'Do you want to have a career as a touring musician or what? No one said it would be easy.'

I bit into my croissant. 'I think I need a break, Haggai. I need to reconfigure how I approach my career and my presence in this city. I always feel like I'm missing something. A code that I can't quite decipher.' I sighed. I was glad for coffee. 'I'm not doing anything in August right now, and I definitely don't want to just hang around New York during the hottest and loneliest month of the year.'

Haggai listened patiently, pulling his ham and cheese croissant into bite-size shreds as I dug myself into a hole. I could feel my chest compressing.

'I love being a musician, and it's all I want to be,' I went on. 'All I want to do is sing, but sometimes I feel like I'm lost – like I've forgotten the rest of me, who I am and who I was before I lived in New York and spent every waking hour obsessing about the meaning of success. I used to be an adventurer, the one who took chances, who didn't think twice, who swam in ice-cold lakes, who climbed mountains, who biked across Europe, who loved without envy, who didn't know fear.'

'Wait – you biked across Europe?' Haggai said, inhaling his coffee and breaking his silence.

'Yeah, years ago now. From London to Gibraltar. I still have that bike, my beautiful red Condor. It gave me some of the greatest experiences of my life,' I told him.

Flecks of featherlight pastry clung to Haggai's beard and shivered as he spoke. 'By all means you should take a holiday, but – I'm sorry to say it – you do need to consider that taking too much time out will mean losing traction with your work.'

'Why can't I just do both? Do we always have to sacrifice half of ourselves for this insane job?' Frustration was rising in me. 'I don't understand why being a musician means being miserable and selfish! Where's the balance? I mean, why can't I do my album release tour on my bike? Screw planes, trains and automobiles – I should just bike the whole thing! It'd be cheaper – and even if the gigs suck, at least I'd have a great adventure.'

Haggai's eyebrows were raised in cautious approval. 'And what about the quartet? Are they going to bike with you too?'

'I'll go solo,' I said defiantly. 'I can play all my songs alone. They'll sound a bit different, but that's okay – it's all or nothing right now.'

'How are you going to carry all your instruments? On your back?' Haggai shook his head and took another sip of coffee.

'No, I have panniers. You know, those bags you clip onto the bike rack. It'll be easy – I can just strap everything to the bike. Tent, clothes, ukulele, loop pedal. Why not?'

'I see, Jo, I see. And where would you want to do this tour?' Haggai led my train of thought along.

I said the first thing that came into my mind: 'How about the West Coast? I've always wanted to bike that route. I bet there are plenty of venues I could play, too.' By now I was starting to believe the idea was genuinely possible. I was excited, my thoughts running faster than I could speak. 'I could probably connect with musicians along the way, and stay with friends. I'll be singing and cycling my way down the West Coast of America! What could be better? I'll call the tour The Great Song Cycle. That's it!' I laughed and looked up at the puffy clouds in the blue sky.

'You know, Jo,' Haggai said, turning his whole body towards me and placing his coffee cup on its saucer, 'I actually know a lot of great musicians on the West Coast. Let me give you their numbers. I think this is a perfect idea.'

We spent the next hour with our phones out, transferring the names and numbers of everyone he could think of – from musicians to yoga studio owners, concert presenters and friends who would be happy to have me stay.

Now that the idea was born, I just had to do it.

Haggai and I embraced at the subway and wished each other a beautiful day. I jogged home across Prospect Park, fuelled by calories and caffeine but also by the excitement of an idea born, an adventure ahead. I opened the door to my studio apartment, the sun streaming through the open windows casting golden lines across the herringbone parquetry floor, and went over to my computer. I sat down and began writing to everyone I knew about my plan: my record label, my manager, my parents. I even emailed some cycling companies to see if they might consider sponsoring me. I figured that the more people I told, the more committed I would be to the task.

After this flurry, I opened Google Maps and zoomed in on the West Coast of America. The only parts I had visited before were Carmel-by-the-Sea, Big Sur and Santa Monica. The rest of the coastline was a mystery to me. I typed

'Seattle' into the search bar and zoomed in to see where
the next major city to the south was. Portland, Oregon.
The route between the two cities, however, looked like a
rather barren few hundred kilometres of road, meaning
there would probably not be many opportunities for me
to perform. So I decided that I would begin this journey
in Portland. Starting from the centre of the city, I panned
south until I came to Santa Monica Pier, in Los Angeles; this
would be my final destination.

'The Great Song Cycle, Portland to LA,' I said aloud,
finding poetry in the words. I said them over again in
my empty apartment until they felt a part of me. Then
I asked Google to calculate the distance between these
two points. It insisted on taking me inland, which was
the shortest and most efficient route, but I wanted to
travel by the coast, so I pulled the blue line over towards
the expanse of ocean and led it, unwaveringly, along
Highway 1. I waited as Google calculated the distance
again, and blinked in surprise as it declared it to be almost
2000 kilometres. I had been preparing myself for at least
twice that distance, so suddenly the whole thing seemed
quite doable.

The next step was to see where I might be able to play
shows, and plan them so that the dates lined up with my
pedal power. I knew I could bike 80 kilometres in a day
without too much trouble, so I zoomed in and found towns
every 80 to 100 kilometres, and then googled 'music venue'.
My planning technique was rough and felt arbitrary, but
soon I fell into a rhythm, and found a surprisingly fruitful
number of places at which I might be able to play a show.
I wrote down the name of each venue, the town it was in,
the distance from the last venue, and made a note about

what kind of space it was: coffee shop, library, yoga studio, concert hall, jazz club, house concert, ukulele store, school.

Step three was to make a decision on *when* I would arrive in these places. This was the most unknowable factor, because it depended entirely on my own willpower, strength and belief that I could actually get there in time. It wasn't like touring by car, where you could easily do a show in one city, drive 100 kilometres north for the next show, 200 kilometres south again, and perhaps another 400 kilometres east, all in four days. This tour would have to be meticulously planned, and every progression had to be in one direction: south.

My official launch show for my album *Gardens In My Mind* was already booked in on the 1st of August at National Sawdust in Williamsburg, featuring my dear friend and pianist, Jesse Elder, and the Solar String Quartet (none of whom are on the original album). I decided this would be the launchpad of The Great Song Cycle, and I would set off westward shortly thereafter. On the 3rd of August I could get a 6 a.m. flight from New York to Portland, and perhaps even find somewhere to play a show that same night. Then I would start cycling on the 4th of August. The dates I was coming up with were random enough, but I had to start somewhere.

In capital letters on a piece of paper I inscribed: 'August 3rd – Day One, Portland, Oregon.' Then I tallied up the number of days it would take me to reach Santa Monica, adding in a few rest days and *who-knows-what-might-happen* days. This calculation brought me through to the 6th of September. Five weeks on the road, alone. I took a deep breath, closed my eyes for a moment and then continued

planning. Zoom in, town, google, music venue, list, pan
south, repeat.

Not four hours since getting out of the pool, I drafted the
email I would send to the various music venues I'd picked
out along the route:

Dear _____,

*My name is Joanna Wallfisch. I am a jazz vocalist
and singer-songwriter.*

*Originally from London, I have lived in New York
since 2010, and over that time I have released three
albums, two of which are on Sunnyside Records, and
the latest, Gardens In My Mind, is being released on
July 22nd of this year.*

*This August I am setting forth on my West Coast
album release tour (Portland–LA), however the
nature of this tour is somewhat different to the usual
'musician on the road', as I will be connecting the
dots of all my shows by bicycle. Hence the title of this
trip: The Great Song Cycle.*

*I am especially looking for intimate concert
settings and community-driven performance
opportunities, which is why I write to you now, as
your venue looks totally perfect for this tour. My
main priority is to draw in the interest of the local
communities as I travel through to share my music
in this less conventional manner, drawing on the
sense of adventure and joie de vivre, fuelled by the
immeasurable power of song itself.*

*I will be passing through _____ around
the ____ of August. Would you have availability
to host my solo show? I will be traveling with my*

ukulele and loop pedal, though I also play the piano, if there is one at the venue. Here is my website: www.joannawallfisch.com.

Thanks for your time, and I look forward to hearing from you.

Joanna

It was guesswork to begin with, and I had no idea if I would ever get through it, but for now I was driven by sheer determination, blissfully ignorant of the reality of what I was getting myself into.

3

THE Q TRAIN

Silence is silver and grey,
Time traces lines with invisible threads.
We walk in our sleep through the day,
And the future exists from the wishes we make.

'When We Travel'

My eyes were burning from hours of staring at my computer, so I closed it and went for a walk. Back down on Ocean Avenue, I was swept along by the perpetual current of life there: my superintendent, Josh, putting out the trash with one hand and waving at me with the other; familiar dog walkers being led by their canines across the street into the park; neighbours straining with bulging sacks of laundry as they returned from the laundromat on Lincoln Road; the smell of burnt bagels wafting from the recently opened bagel shop; pigeons lifting from the street, narrowly avoiding certain death from cars that accelerated too fast between the lights; the man who slept in a makeshift home of drums and tarpaulin on the bench across the street.

I rounded the corner of my yellow building, my mind 4000 kilometres away, and found myself on the Manhattan-bound platform of Prospect Park subway station. The Q train pulled up, the doors opening with a familiar *bing*, and I stepped on. I found riding the subway in the middle of the day strangely calming. The car was only half-full, and it was unusually quiet. People were sitting reading books or staring into the middle distance. I loved being a stranger among strangers, feeling a sense of family without a name.

My thoughts could dance freely with the rhythm of the moving train.

Within moments, the train plunged through the tunnel towards 7th Avenue and my phone lost signal. I stood in the middle of the carriage, surfing the subway as it sped around corners and pulled in at stop after stop. After DeKalb Avenue, the train slowly pulled out of the tunnel once more and onto Manhattan Bridge. The sun poured over the East River, casting long shadows from Brooklyn Bridge to the south and Williamsburg Bridge to the north, lighting the grey water with diamonds. The south end of Manhattan towered like Emerald City and I stood glued to the window, looking past the scratched-on love hearts and greasy handprints. I remembered why I loved this city so much.

Nearing the end of the bridge, the train passed over the graffitied rooftops of China Town. Even through the closed doors I could smell the exotic scents rising up from the historical quarter. Ten minutes later we pulled in at Union Square and I got off. Music drew me up the steps and, prevailing over the entire floor above, a crowd of commuters, willing to miss their trains, surrounded a dancer wearing a fuchsia-coloured, sequinned, skintight mini-dress, with platform shoes to match. With lithe arms and legs to die for, he was twirling, flowing, kicking and spinning like a peacock on heat to the strains of Aretha Franklin's 'Respect'. People cheered and threw dollar bills into the suitcase he had open against the filthy white-tiled wall, but he ignored them, maintaining his fierce diva attitude as he increased the speed of his twirls and deepened the gyrations of his gorgeous hips.

I pushed through the gate and exited into the sunshine of Union Square. Chess players called for brave opponents, the farmers' market bustled with wealthy shoppers, and

I stood there watching. I had done this countless times before, but this time I sensed that something had shifted, that a major life change was in the making.

I dug in my pocket for my phone, my thumb automatically pressing on the mailbox icon. A flurry of new messages filled my inbox: to my surprise, many were from the venues I had emailed only a few hours before. I was accustomed to waiting days, if not weeks, before hearing back from a venue about playing a show. Many of them were positive: 'Yes, we'd love to have you play at our venue.' I even had an email from Ortlieb USA, one of the best bicycle luggage companies in the world, which I'd contacted about getting sponsorship. 'Whatever you need,' they offered. I punched the air, yelped loudly into the crowd and did a twirl of my own. Nobody seemed to notice.

By now I was fizzing with new purpose. My harebrained idea was gaining momentum, and soon I was piecing together a great puzzle. I spent the rest of the day walking through Manhattan, plotting how the journey could work. I walked until night fell and finally returned home, exhausted but elated. From this point on, The Great Song Cycle was never out of my mind.

As the weeks moved on and August drew nearer, I had my first glimmer of doubt. The gigs were almost all booked but I had barely started training, as I'd been spending so many hours on the computer. I began to realise the mammoth undertaking ahead of me. One sunny afternoon, my hands cramped over my keyboard, my eyes bloodshot from hours of staring at the blue light, I threw a post up on Facebook:

'Who out there loves biking, camping, music and wants to go on an adventure? If that sounds like you, send me a message.'

I wasn't so sure I wanted to do this alone anymore. Something inside me knew I needed a riding buddy – if for no other reason than to keep me accountable to the plan, no matter how afraid of it I was becoming.

A moment later my phone rang. It was my friend Joel. I picked up and he said, 'I do!'

'Oh, hi, Joel,' I answered, not sure what he meant. 'How's it going?'

'Fine, thanks. So, about your post – I want to go on an adventure!'

I had known Joel for little over a year. We had met at Mona's, a tiny galley-bar on the Lower East Side. He played the double bass in the bluegrass band on Monday nights. I had gone there one winter's night with my best friend, Julia, and after hours of dancing and whisky I had gone home with Joel. It was a fumbling, awkward and comical encounter, which concluded at dawn when he revealed he was already seeing somebody. I wasn't surprised – this was New York, after all – so I simply rolled my eyes and put the kettle on. We'd run into each other on the local music scene a number of times after that and somehow become friends, without a hint of romance beyond.

'Okay,' I said. 'Have you ever ridden a bike before?' I had never considered him an outdoor type, and I was sure he was joking.

He laughed. 'Of course! I ride almost every day.'

'Okay…And what kind of bike do you have?' I continued, interview-style.

'I have a great single-speed with a basket on the handlebars for luggage.'

'Okay. And what's the most you've ever ridden in a single day?' I started taking notes.

'I ride loops around Prospect Park most days. So probably about twelve miles.'

'You do realise what I am planning to do, right? Bike the whole of the West Coast, without vehicle support, playing shows along the way. I'll be camping, and carrying probably about thirty kilos of luggage on the bike.'

'Yeah, I know. I guess.'

'Well,' I sighed, 'we should probably meet for coffee and discuss this properly. If you're serious, then you're going to have to get a new bike and do a ton of training. Oh, and Joel,' I paused. 'I hope this isn't some weird way to, you know, get in my pants.' I hung up.

We met the next morning in the park. He rode towards me on his vintage single-speed, a wicker basket holding a satchel and his helmet strap hanging loose. I was not optimistic.

'There are a few things you should be prepared for, aside from fitness and a new bike. This isn't going to be a bunch of roses. I am foreseeing this trip as one of the hardest things I've ever done before.' I told Joel as we sat cross-legged on the grass, his old bike lying on the ground, pedals akimbo, like a dead dog. 'I can get grumpy too! I just want to warn you, because there's already a lot of pressure without having to be nice all the time.'

Two weeks later, I got a text message from him with a photo of a beautiful brand-new Trek touring bike and a set of gleaming blue Ortlieb pannier bags, along with a message: 'I am riding to Oak Hill NY this weekend for the blues festival. It's a 350-mile round trip.'

I guess he really wanted an adventure.

4

STARTING GUN

Holding hands, closing eyes,
Check in lines, long goodbyes,
The in-flight service includes broken hearts.

'In Flight Service'

BROOKLYN – PORTLAND: 4000 KILOMETRES

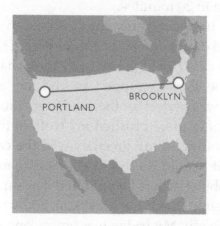

It was the 3rd of August 2016, and the shrill radar setting on my alarm went off at 4 a.m., rebounding off the walls of my studio apartment and settling on my eardrums without apology. What my alarm didn't know was that I was already awake, and had been since 3 a.m., quietly waiting for this affronting noise to force me up and into the unknown. I'd had little time to celebrate the triumph of my concert at National Sawdust just two nights earlier, and had found it difficult to sleep, still buzzing from adrenaline. With the sheets up to my nose, I raised my eyes and looked out of the window above my pillow. I slept with my curtains open so that I could see the moon. The sky was a dark, grimy orange, and the fire escape cut an iconic Brooklyn silhouette into the dawn.

Blinking through the gloom, I looked towards the neatly packed sports bag beside my bed, to which I'd strapped my helmet and ukulele case. Inside were all the contents I would need to survive for the next five weeks. My bike was already waiting for me in Portland; I had shipped it via a FedEx service called Bike Flights two weeks earlier. My taxi would arrive in 20 minutes.

I stalled, unmoving, my mind a broken dam flooded with fear and doubt. *I don't have to do this, do I? Would anyone mind if I just didn't go?* But my body took charge, carefully unfolding the sheets wrapped around me, and remaking the bed so it was perfect for the sub-letter who would arrive in a couple of hours. I brushed my teeth in the white-tiled bathroom, staring at my green eyes in the cabinet mirror, wondering if I could do this at all. Placing my toothbrush inside the cabinet, where I would find it again on my return, I wiped the sink, closed the toilet seat, and straightened the towels on the rail. My fridge was empty and clean, though the kitchen sink remained a hub for the nightly New York cockroach conference.

I closed the windows, slipped on my loose-fitting travel clothes, picked up my compact world and slung it over my shoulder. After taking a last look at my tiny home, I opened the heavy fireproof door and walked out into the brightly lit hallway of the old tenement building. The only sign of life was the off-beat peeping of the broken smoke alarm on the stairs. I pressed the call button on the elevator, then closed and locked my teal-green door behind me. Getting into the brass-walled elevator, inscribed with graffiti and the smell of urine, the bulb blinking in time with my heart,

I descended. Downstairs, I walked across the terracotta tiles and out into the new day. Nobody saw me leave.

Dawn lifted in a sheet of powder blue behind the silhouette of the trees in Prospect Park. The air was cool and sweet, yet to be weighed down by the smog of a summer's day in New York City.

'To JFK, please,' I told the taxi driver. With a nod of his head, we drove down Ocean Avenue, away from my yellow building, passed the first joggers of the day, along Flatbush Avenue and deep into the red-bricks of Brooklyn.

Checking in for a flight had never been easier. I had no computer in my hand luggage, only my ukulele and bike helmet, my journal, my passport, phone and wallet. The airport was like and unlike every other. Tired and wan faces waiting, queuing, shuffling forward, shoes off, liquids out, hands up, belts off, bags open, phones out, pockets empty, X-ray, pat down, faceless bodies, numbers, all in limbo between coming and going. Overpriced food wrapped in disposable packaging filling the stomachs of a thousand strangers. Everyone was on a journey somewhere – for work, for play, for new beginnings, for escape. I felt like a sardine following the current, invisible amid the ebb and flow of the domestic terminal.

On the plane, I closed my eyes and leant my head against the oval window, hooking my feet into the magazine pocket on the seat in front of me. The morning sun pierced white against my closed eyelids, igniting a deep-red curtain, its warmth refracting through the double-glazed window and warming my cheek. Before we left the ground, sleep took over. I was on my way to Portland and, as if I had dreamt the whole flight, we landed just as I opened my eyes.

Dan and Danielle met me off the Red Line train in Beaverton, Portland. I had yet to meet them in person, though we had chatted via email a number of times during the planning stages of my tour. They were generously hosting my inaugural concert, which would be held that same evening in their backyard. Joel had arrived in Portland the night before and had stayed in a cheap hotel. He would make his own way, via a chain of coffee shops, to Aaron Brook's house, where our bicycles were waiting, and where we would meet in the next couple of hours. It was a day of convergence: we were tributaries running towards a great ocean.

Aaron was a bicycle mechanic who, a month earlier, happened to answer the phone when I called a bike shop in Portland, looking for somewhere to FedEx our bicycles to. The quote from the store to receive and rebuild our bikes was way over $100 each, but Aaron, adjusting his customer service bellow to a conspiratorial whisper, told me that he had a private shop in his yard and would do both bikes for $100. For reasons that are neither rational nor intelligent, I trusted him, took down his address and sent our priceless steeds to his home in Portland.

Weeks later, as Dan and I pulled up outside his home, my heart was beating with anticipation. An impressive grapevine formed a welcoming arch for us to walk under. Joel was already there, and stood smiling next to his bike as Aaron gave my shining Condor the final touches, making sure everything was tight, greased and ready for the long journey ahead. Looking up from his work, he greeted me with a toothy grin and, after wiping bike grease from his hands on a rag, shook my hand. A blond five o'clock shadow prickled on his round chin; a naked woman was printed on his tattered T-shirt.

'You've got a fun ride ahead of you,' he said, smiling, as he handed me my bike. 'The weather's going to be perfect!'

Ecstatic to be reunited with my bike, and amazed that my plan so far had worked out, I gave Aaron a hundred-dollar bill, plus $20 as tip, and we loaded our bikes into Dan's van and drove to our first concert of the tour.

Four Douglas fir trees stretched into the summer sky, forming an intimate amphitheatre around us. Friends and neighbours congregated amid the citronella candles and snacks. Joel and I played a concert of songs that we had rehearsed back in Brooklyn – Joel on bass and me on a concert ukulele and loop pedal – to smiling faces and generous applause. The Great Song Cycle had officially commenced in the form of song, though the cycling had yet to start. That would begin first thing tomorrow morning.

For now, we basked in the soft evening light, drinking wine and sharing songs and stories with new friends. Only this morning I had woken in Brooklyn unsure if I would even leave my apartment, and now, barely eighteen hours later, I was singing to the cicadas in Oregon.

At 7 a.m. the next morning I knocked on Joel's door. He was grumpy and in pain. The inflatable bed he'd been sleeping on had deflated and left him sleepless on a hardwood floor. Exhausted from the previous day, I had slept like a baby in the next room on a soft queen-sized bed, thick with down pillows and a heavy duvet. I was in a great mood and ready to lead us on our way south.

Eggs were cooking and fresh coffee was brewing in the kitchen. Everything this morning dripped with symbolism. I showered – my last shower before I biked to LA. Over breakfast, I announced: 'This is our last breakfast before we bike to LA!' Berries, avocados, orange juice, toast, jam, tomatoes. Every bite a symbol of the unknown and the possible. We gorged on breakfast and conversation, and as the waistband on my lycra shorts started to dig into my full belly, I looked at the clock. No more procrastinating: it was time to go.

Straddling our heavily loaded bikes, Joel and I posed for a photo. We were dressed in fluorescent T-shirts that I had adorned with bubble-paint, spelling out 'THE GREAT SONG CYCLE, PORTLAND TO LA'. I felt dizzy with anticipation. My body was strong from the training I had done over the last couple of months back in New York: riding upstate every couple of weekends, the odd jog around the park and my daily swimming routine. But as the day of departure had grown closer, I'd fallen into a spell of denial and barely trained at all. I knew that nothing could really prepare me for what lay ahead: riding over 1500 kilometres, hauling 35 kilograms of luggage. The real training was about to begin.

We waved Dan and Danielle goodbye and rolled away cautiously, wobbling as we got used to the weight of our bikes, down the hill and around the first bend. I was smiling from ear to ear, my helmet secure, my cycling shades firmly on the bridge of my nose, and the scent of sunscreen mingling with the morning air. The sky was clear and blue, cool and breezy.

Testing the manoeuvrability of my front wheel, which was also loaded with two well-packed panniers, I discovered that I was actually pretty stable on this vehicle.

Ortlieb had provided me with five bright-yellow bags: two for the back rack, two for the front, and one that would sit between my handlebars. I looked like a giant yellow hamster on wheels, its pouches full to bursting. The sound of the tarmac hummed soothingly beneath my tyres, sending a shiver of excitement through my bones. This would be my soundtrack for the next month.

Happy and free, I called out to the sky and road ahead, 'Off we go!'

At that moment we passed the only other people around, a woman walking hand-in-hand with her young daughter. 'Where are you going?' she called back, as if I were talking to her.

'To Los Angeles!' I said, the words sounding comical, given our starting point.

Her eyes widened, her face opened into a glorious smile and she cried out, as she fist-pumped the air, 'You rock!'

Her daughter looked up quizzically at her mum and we all laughed. Her words in that moment were the starting gun for The Great Song Cycle.

5

WARM SHOWERS

PORTLAND – SALEM – EUGENE: 210 KILOMETRES

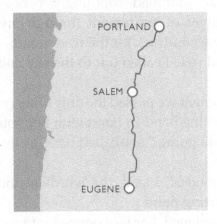

With a smooth road and a clear day, it felt like we were the only ones travelling this way. We had set ourselves an easy goal to start the journey: 87 kilometres from the Portland suburb of Beaverton to the town of Salem. We concentrated on the small roads that wove through the farmlands of Oregon, leaving the roar of the traffic behind us. It was easy to fall into a false sense of security that we'd be able to do this the whole way to LA. Every few miles we were spoilt with offerings from local farm stands, and we gorged on golden, juicy peaches, cherries and plums, and homemade ice cream.

'So, Jo, where are we staying tonight?' Joel asked casually.

I hadn't booked any accommodation in Salem, and had somehow forgotten this key detail until now. Before I lost phone signal, I logged into a new app I'd found, called Warm Showers. It's a free app, similar to Couchsurfing but dedicated to hosting those travelling by bicycle. It was easy enough to use. Each town had a number of red drop-pins, and each drop-pin signified a host. I zoomed in on the pins around Salem until I came across a name that also said 'currently hosting'. I opened a profile belonging to Chris and Sarah, and wrote them a message.

'Dear Chris and Sarah, I am riding from Portland to Salem today with my friend Joel and we wanted to ask if there is a possibility you might have room for us to stay tonight? I know it's short notice. I don't have much phone signal, so I will check back in a couple of hours. Best, Jo.'

Just as I was repacking my phone it rang. 'Hi, is that Jo? It's Chris here.' A kind, deep baritone voice sounded on the other end of the line.

'Hi, yes, it is. Thanks for getting back to me so quickly.'

'You're both welcome to stay here tonight. What's your ETA?' he said, matter-of-factly.

And just like that we had our home for the night.

We rolled into Salem in the early evening. My stomach was cramping and bloated from dehydration and eating too many energy bars. I had been carrying two water bottles, planning to fill them up often, but the only place we'd passed was a truck depot. We rolled our bikes through the large lot of behemoth vehicles and up to the small office to ask if we could refill our bottles there.

'It's against our policy,' the receptionist told us, her thickly mascaraed eyelashes unblinking.

'What? It's against your policy to let two dehydrated cyclists, whose next stop isn't for thirty miles, fill up their bottles with water? What kind of policy is that?' I was outraged.

'You can purchase bottled water from the vending machines outside,' she said, her expression unmoving.

'But we don't have cash, and we're desperately thirsty,'
I pushed. Behind low grey walls, thick-necked men in
sweat-stained white shirts and red ties looked up over their
computer screens. One stood up and walked over to us.
'Anything I can help you with?' he asked, looking me up
and down, his eyes lingering on my legs. He ignored Joel
altogether.

'Yes,' I said. 'Your receptionist has refused to give us any
water and we're desperate.'

'It's against our policy to give water to the general
public,' he said, his voice cold.

I heard a snigger from behind one of the partitions, and
we walked out of the office in a fury, bottles empty.

We arrived about an hour after the time I'd told Chris,
and when we reached their house he was waiting on the
verandah with a fatherly look of concern on his face. In his
late sixties, Chris was tall, with strong, tanned arms from
his gardening passion. Through his bushy white eyebrows
grey eyes shone out with the complexity of labradorite.
Sarah appeared on the other side of the front door, her
rosy cheeks beaming through a lace curtain draped over
the large window pane. Chris mumbled something about
being hungry as he'd only eaten carrots all day. Sarah
ushered us in with matronly warmth.

They lived in a large craftsman house with the original
mouldings still intact. We wheeled our bikes into the wide
entrance hall, and without any fuss they showed us upstairs
to our rooms. My legs complained as I climbed the stairs so
I held on to the banister with the determination of a three-
year-old tackling them for the first time. I was given a small
room at the front of the house, with an ornate mahogany
bed in the centre of the room, adorned with a Victorian
patchwork quilt. Joel was in the twin room down the hall.

Chris and Sarah patiently waited as we indulged in what we had been promised all along: warm showers. I used the downstairs bathroom, which had a shower that sprayed from every angle imaginable. Stepping into the ocean-mosaic-tiled shower stand, I looked down at my distended stomach and throbbing legs. They felt like they were not my own. I closed my eyes and let the hot water run down my back and down the drain, along with the kilometres, the layers of sunscreen and sweat.

Chris and Sarah took us for Thai food, their treat. Conversation rolled as easily as we had along the flat roads of Oregon. Joel and I exchanged the occasional glance: *Is this really happening? This is too good to be true!*

Everybody else seemed energised from the meal but my strength was fading fast, and as soon as we got home I excused myself and went to bed. I sighed into the silence and leaned into the bliss of being alone. I listened in the darkness; I hadn't heard quiet like this for months, if not years. My eardrums were still reverberating with the intense decibels of New York City and my flight across the country the day before. I fell hard into a dreamless sleep.

In the morning we thanked Chris and Sarah for their generous hospitality and headed to a cafe called Word of Mouth – the local brunch spot. Joel and I ordered enough food to feed a family of five, plus two veggie burgers and fries for lunch. I had an omelette with potatoes, a side of avocado, freshly squeezed orange juice and bottomless coffee. We ate outside on a dilapidated picnic table, our bikes leaning up against the wall. Next to our coffee cups was a pile of gloves, sunglasses and helmets.

We ate until we could hardly move, and before setting off I carefully stuffed a veggie burger into each of my front panniers. My stomach was still feeling tender but I wanted to make sure I had enough fuel to get me through the day. Joel and I had argued about biking to Eugene in a single day – 120 kilometres. He thought it was too far, but I insisted that if we managed that distance in one day, then we could reward ourselves with a full day off to rest and explore the city.

Understanding how to eat for long-distance biking was a steep learning curve for both of us, and it wasn't until later that day, under the shade of a large tree in the lot of a more friendly trucking company, that I realised eating large meals during the day was a terrible idea. Woozy and sluggish from the heat, I struggled to swallow the food we had brought with us, finding it repeating on me as we peddled on. My body was on a strange sort of roller-coaster. Intense hunger and exhaustion would strike, bringing dizziness and a foul mood; to remedy this, I would stop and gorge, which would in turn initiate at least an hour of lethargy and painful digestion. Joel and I decided there'd be no more huge meals like that while we were riding. We would eat only snacks through the day, and then look forward to a big dinner.

By mid-afternoon, a glorious tailwind picked up and swept us along at an average of almost 30 kilometres per hour through the rolling hills towards the Willamette River. Joel and I biked in convivial silence, lost in our own thoughts. Occasionally the silence was broken by the sound of our voices rising in song as we regaled each other with our favourite jazz standards to pass the time.

The sun was relentless, the tailwind bountiful, and I hadn't felt a drop of sweat on my forehead all day. Every ounce of extra fluid I had drunk had evaporated into thin air. We were nearing Eugene, and as the miles decreased, so too did our senses of humour.

The early evening settled like a gentle kiss, the iridescent light dappling through the trees cast a tessellation of shadows upon the road ahead of us. I stared at the shapes, hypnotised by their dance.

Finally, we crossed the bridge over the Willamette River, taking us into the outskirts of Eugene. I called out to Joel: 'We're going swimming!'

I signalled and turned right, following a path that led through a campground and steeply down to the water's edge. We wheeled our bikes down the dirt path and leaned them against a tree stump. My bathing suit was buried at the bottom of my luggage but I had no patience to dig for it so, taking off only my shoes, I walked into the icy water in my cycling shorts and sports bra. My feet sank into the strange softness of mud and algae-covered stones, and the cold water wrapped around my swollen legs, reaching up around my thighs, crotch and stomach, the strong current pulling me in. I lifted my feet, submerged my head and was swept downriver.

My mind tingled with new clarity as each mile of the day floated downstream with the current. I laughed out loud into the clear water. Opening my arms, I slowed myself and found, just beneath the surface, a tree root I could wrap my toes around. Once secure, I lay back in the water and, like Ophelia, floated in the arms of the golden-green river, my hair splayed around me like long grass.

Just after 7 p.m., eleven hours after leaving Salem, we crawled up the final hill of the day. My GPS directed us to a small white cottage on the corner of the hill. Using my last ounce of strength, I heaved my bike into the driveway, Joel right behind me. It seemed no one was home, but I had instructions in an email from Svevo to enter through the back gate. If he wasn't home, he'd said, we should just come in – 'the back door will be open'.

Through the back gate I saw a hot tub. I opened the gate and approached the back door. It was dark inside, so I pressed my nose against the glass to try to see inside. All of a sudden a large husky appeared on the other side of the glass and stuck its nose against mine. Jumping back, Joel asked me what was wrong.

'I'm not sure this is the right house,' I said.

'Are you sure? Svevo said we could just let ourselves in, right?' Joel asked.

'Hmm.' I tried the door; it was open. As soon as I pushed it ajar, the husky started to bark fiercely. I slammed it closed and swiftly we retreated. I looked at the number on the front door and realised that we had in fact arrived at the wrong address.

We got back on our bikes and dug deep for one more push to the very top of the road, where we reached the house we were looking for. High on the hill, surrounded by trees and vines, was a cedar house that looked like a ship on the high seas. The side door was nestled in the bushes and behind it was a steep staircase.

'Hello?' I called out. 'Svevo?' He was an old family friend of a friend of a friend, and I'd never met him before. I didn't know if he was young or old, or even how to pronounce his name.

'Jo?' a bright voice called back. 'Come in, come in!'

Svevo came bounding down the steps to greet us. His smile was the first thing I noticed: a radiant, toothy grin that lifted his eyes into half-moons, surrounded by a vast forest of wrinkles. He wore nothing but a pair of thin hemp trousers, held up by a belt made of rope. Beneath his bony chest, his bare, tanned stomach protruded like a yogi's. His hair spun out wildly in all directions, a mess of auburn and grey, and his hands were a complex map of a life well lived. Svevo's home was like the inside of a majestic but wizened oak tree. Everything was made of wood, and the only soft furnishings were a large futon in the open-plan living room and two worn floor-cushions.

We were famished. Svevo had boiled some beets, baby potatoes and picked green beans and blackberries from his garden. We ate this modest but perfectly formed meal out of small wooden bowls, sitting on the floor next to the large window. In the time it took for the evening sunlight to pirouette across the wooden floor in golden streamers and fade to darkness, we had become friends.

I had planned to keep a journal throughout the tour, but as it turned out I was so exhausted most days that I barely wrote. I found it worked better for me to record voice memos on my phone as I biked along. But after this day of cycling I was inspired to put pen to paper, for the first and last time, to express the awe I was feeling.

> *Lying on a hammock in Svevo's garden. It is slung low and I can feel the grass tickling my back through the knotted rope. It is silent, still, the evening is settling in perfectly and I couldn't be happier or feel*

more at peace with the situation. Today I biked 76 miles from Salem to Eugene. Joel has so far been a super companion. Encouraging, supportive and just good company. A bee is buzzing beneath me in the grass. Svevo keeps bees and I just dug out some 20-year-old comb honey from a giant jar with a wooden spoon. My arms are almost too tired to hold this pen to write. This is day two of my trip. I've not yet quite counted exactly how many I have ahead altogether…why should I? The days will happen.

Today was super. Very long, setting off after breakfast at 8.47 a.m., and finally arriving at 7.05 p.m. But we took many breaks, including a swim in a river. What a feeling to walk into a cold, rushing river at mile 65 and feel your whole hot and sore, tired body almost sizzle as it meets the water. Pure heaven. This is heaven. I am amazed also at how easy it is, once you decide to go, and then just go, to make an adventure like this happen.

You have to be very open and happy to take each moment as it comes. Life on a bicycle teaches you to go with the flow, but also reveals the flexibility of time and space. Your expectations and limitations change, your perception of distance too. Yesterday the plan was 54 miles, so by mile 50 we were tired. Today, 76 miles and by mile 50 you felt happy that there were only 26 miles to go. Everything, it turns out, is relative…

Bats and cicadas, a distant train whistles, sweet evening air. The sky melting into a crystal mauve. Bearing witness to the full spectrum of a day…what a privilege.

We had earned our day off in Eugene, and took relaxation very seriously. I woke up in Svevo's home in a small room with a window that overlooked the woods beyond the house. The three of us enjoyed a peaceful and slow-moving breakfast of hand-ground oats soaked in beet-water, with berries picked from the garden, sprinkled with chopped banana, raisins and a glob of almond butter. Svevo then presented us with tea made from cedar bark that he had collected from the woods.

After our foragers' breakfast, Joel and I took a walk into town to explore. We found a spot to get some delicious coffee and avocado toast. There was a sense of celebration in everything, from acknowledging the sweetly scented trees that lined the streets, the old craftsman houses, the fast-flowing river, to the prospect of fresh coffee and a second breakfast. Everything in slow motion, we sat and observed as the world passed us by, reflecting on our inaugural days on the road and trying not to dwell on the many miles still ahead of us.

We spent the rest of the sunny afternoon on the banks of the Willamette River, where we swam, read and mostly did nothing. There were a few other people gathered on the flat, warm rocks – a group of young students enjoying a carefree summer afternoon, a solitary bare-chested guy swirling in a pot-induced stupor under a tree, gently swaying and murmuring into the dappled shadows. And then, as if out of the rocks themselves, an old man appeared.

He was shirtless, his leathery skin hanging like dried fish from his arms, his skinny pot-belly pushing his filthy jeans so low that the top of his hairy groin was barely sheltered beneath the worn-out denim. His long beard was fashioned in a skinny braid and snaked from his chin to meet with the grey curlicue wisps upon his pigeon-chest. Out of his backpack he took a ream of colourful strings. He did everything with the precision and elegance of a magician. With this same care and mystery, he began tying these rainbow threads in elaborate knots onto a low branch of a tree that stretched out from the rocks beneath the clear water. He was a combination of so many things: a child, an old man, an enigma and an open book.

Every so often he would walk into the water up to his ankles, looking down as if hoping to find treasure. He was also unabashedly eavesdropping on the conversation Joel and I were having as he turned to us to smile, nod and sometimes, hunching up his coat-hanger shoulders, giggle. Then he pulled out a pipe and appeared to melt something dark and sticky with his lighter into the bellow, and inhaled whatever was inside.

His stance and posture immediately changed. Abandoning his colourful threads, he sat down on his backpack, knees bent to his ears, and dropped his head in his hands. Sometimes he would lift his eyes above his fingers, his dull eyeballs darting left to right, as if he were a child playing hide-and-seek, but the only hiding place he could find was behind his own eyelids. We left him there beside the cool, rushing river and wandered back to Svevo's.

The early evening was spent in simple quietness. We returned to Svevo's armed with goodies for dinner, including some locally brewed beers and not-so-locally made ice cream. Accompanied by the sweet and heady smell of baking bread, we tinkered with our bikes and repacked our panniers. Svevo humbly pulled fresh out of the Aga two round, pink loaves of bread that he had made using the same sourdough culture he acquired fifty years ago from an old friend and water from boiled beetroots. The loaves sang as the steam rose from the crisscrosses on top. When he sliced into the larger loaf, the dough leaned with the knife and then sprang back to its spongy, welcoming form.

I poured a pool of deep-green olive oil onto a wooden plate and took a hunk of bread to the hammock outside, enjoying another moment of pure stillness and bliss. Even a few days into this trip I could sense myself slowing down, becoming more a part of the present moment, both internally and externally.

As night fell, a strange sound echoed from the trees above in the woods beyond the garden. It was a familiar yet also completely alien noise. A man's voice, warbling in true operatic form at the top of his lungs, seemed to come from the midst of the forest. At first I thought it was somebody's TV, or perhaps a neighbour singing in the shower. Over dinner I asked Svevo what it could be.

'Oh, that's the Opera Singer,' Svevo said, his moon eyes turning up in a smile. 'He's out there most nights. No one ever sees him, but he spends the night in the forest singing. He probably thinks he's a werewolf. Either way, he's harmless.'

Mingling with the constant chirp of cicadas, the singer's voice pierced through like a phantom, and rang through the night until dawn.

6

PAIN IN THE NECK

EUGENE – COTTAGE GROVE – REEDSPORT: 167 KILOMETRES

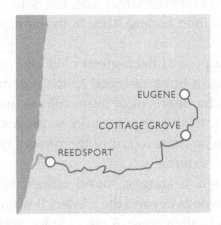

Sleep did not come easy that night. I lay awake looking up at the stars as they blinked through the open window above the silhouetted forest. I listened as the 'opera singer' began each new and unrecognisable aria. I was barely 200 kilometres into the journey and already I was exhausted. The days and distances that lay ahead remained an overwhelming mystery. The landscape was unknown. The concerts were unknown. The places I would sleep were unknown and unplanned. The same anxiety from three days earlier in Brooklyn started to creep back in through the half-light.

Then came a knock on my door. Joel, too, was sleepless, so I welcomed him into the room and under my thin blanket. Curling up on my futon, we looked at each other, nose to nose.

'This can't be anything more than friendship, you know,' I said, unblinking.

'I know. That's cool,' Joel responded, as our hands found each other and our lips met in a kiss.

At 3 a.m. he returned to his own room and I finally fell into a deep, if truncated sleep. I woke at 7 a.m. to the sounds of Svevo and Joel chatting jovially, and the smell of coffee. I felt sluggish and grumpy, a layer of regret on my skin. I took my new sundress, which I had bought at a thrift store the day before, into the small green bathroom, laid it on the sink with my underwear and earrings, and showered. 'Hurry up,' Joel called through the door.

I started to rush. Stepping out of the shower, the soap barely rinsed from my skin, I towelled off and flipped my long, wet hair forwards to wrap the towel around my head. I lifted my head with a flick, and all of a sudden a screaming pain flooded my neck, shoulders and skull. I stood there, naked and frozen, bent at a 45-degree angle, my neck in a spasm and throbbing with needles.

'Fuck, fuck, fuck, fuck!' I spat under my breath, glancing over at myself in the mirror, eyebrows furrowed and lips pursed. Locking eyes with myself, I willed myself to an upright standing position, then, taking a deep breath, I gingerly attempted to move my neck. It wouldn't budge, at least not without the sensation of hot pokers being bored through my spine. 'Fuck,' I said again, and let out a whimper, then a sigh, then a grunt.

I wasn't going to let this get in the way of everything I had planned for today. We had to be at the Eugene farmers' market in thirty minutes to play a set, and then we'd be biking 56 kilometres to Cottage Grove for another show tonight at the Axe and Fiddle.

Slowly lifting my arms, I removed the towel and combed my fingers through my wet hair. Keeping my eyes locked on the mirror, I reached carefully for my underwear and stepped into it, not moving my head all the while. Very cautiously I reached for the dress, dropped it over my head, tucked my arms into the sleeves and pulled it over my body, then straightened up. Step one – I was dressed. Step two was to find the strongest pain reliever I could, and take a double dose. Joel had been knocking back Aleve every few hours since Beaverton for his chronic knee problems, so I knew I had access to the good stuff.

Svevo drove us in his red Volvo down to the house of Sam Peterson, a local musician who was graciously lending Joel his bass for the gig. I smiled through the pain as we gathered in the living room of Sam's cottage and collected the instrument that was almost as tall as his ceilings. It was a brilliant summery Saturday morning. The myriad market stalls were set up and in full swing, draped with colourful clothes, artisanal jewellery and foods from around the world. There was a children's entertainer dressed in tie-dye and suspenders on the stage; in front of him, a small gathering of bemused kids watched as he sang clownish songs on his out-of-tune guitar.

We were up next, and waited backstage for our turn to soundcheck. Just then a friend of Svevo's arrived. Her name was Janette; we'd enjoyed a light meal with her on Svevo's patio the evening before. There was a beaming smile upon her plum-stained lips as she took my hand with both of hers, looked me dead in the eyes and placed a gift into my palms. I didn't have to look to know what it was, its scent rising and making me sweetly dizzy. In my hands was about $300 worth of the finest organic, home-grown weed.

'My son grows it,' she told me. 'I thought it might come in useful for your journey. Even if you don't smoke it, you can probably trade it for shelter or food on your way down the coast.'

I hugged Janette. 'That's amazing, thank you,' I said, tucking the bag of green into my ukulele case.

My neck and shoulders had started to loosen and the pain began to ease just in time for our set. We played to an attentive audience, and in the crowd I was surprised to see two faces I recognised. Exactly one week before, during my album launch show in New York, I'd told the audience that I would be heading to Oregon to begin my album tour – by bicycle. After the show, a man in a floral shirt had approached me.

'I live in Eugene,' he told me. 'When will you be there?'

'Really? All being well, I'll be there next Saturday to play at the farmers' market. You should come!'

I had spoken blithely, never expecting he would show. But now, in the front row, wearing shorts and sunglasses, he waved and sang along with the songs he'd heard seven days and 4000 kilometres away.

After our set, a woman in her sixties approached me and said, 'Hi, Joanna, I'm Silas's mum! He told me you'd be here!' She was the mother of one of my besties from New York, and we embraced as though we, too, were old friends.

The pain in my neck evaporated, leaving only the fizzing sensation of hope and positivity, sparked by the support I had already been shown by complete strangers in these first few days on the road. Everything felt possible once again.

Joel and I packed up our instruments and, before we left the market and said goodbye to everybody, stocked up on some cycling essentials: purple and green beans, apples, cherry tomatoes, almonds, and a small weed pipe made from stone found in the Willamette River (or so I was told by the two baked guys who sold it to me).

Our bikes were waiting for us in Svevo's garage. After changing from my sundress to lycra, and caking my freshly soaped skin with sunscreen, I said farewell to Svevo, thanking him for his hospitality. His moon eyes shone bright as he thanked us both in return.

As soon as I got on my bike and leaned on the handlebars, though, the pain in my neck burst through once again, taking my breath away. 'Shit, Joel, I don't know if I can ride at all,' I said, my voice quavering.

'Why don't we just try a mile or so?' he replied. 'If it's really no good, Svevo could probably drive us the rest of the way.'

'I don't want to be driven. I want to ride. I can't give up already!' I said stubbornly.

Taking a deep breath to fill the very bottom of my lungs with calming air, I rolled down the steep hill we had crawled up two days earlier, my fingers pulling on the brakes, my toes digging into the ends of my shoes against the pain. One way or another, we were back on the road.

I couldn't turn my head in either direction, though, and could barely even move my eyes, so I fixed them on the front of my wheel. I bit my lip and groaned into the seat, my shoulders burning as I tensed up with tears. We had barely ridden for five minutes when I cried out, 'I think we have to stop! I don't think I can make it to Cottage Grove.'

Saying this out loud took all my effort. I was admitting defeat. We pushed our bikes off the road and wheeled along the sidewalk to a bodega, where I got a bag of potato chips and a coke. I sat down on the curb and Joel stood a few feet away, hands on his hips, looking out towards the highway.

The dust and the smell of petroleum stung my nose, and I filled up on sugar and greasy chips in silence. I meditated on whether, if I were alone and had no other choice, I would actually be able to get myself the 56 kilometres to Cottage Grove after all. Standing up carefully, my blood-sugar levels boosted, I put my helmet back on and said, 'Let's go.'

Joel rode close behind me, and acted as the eyes for both of us. If we had to make a left turn, he would look behind and as soon as he called out, 'All clear – go, go, go,' I would put all my trust in him and steer half-blind across the lanes. I was unable to lift my arm to signal, and I couldn't look in any direction other than forward.

Within a stressful hour we were off Highway 5 and once again on small, car-free roads gliding through open farmland and past impressive homes. We developed a system of communication: Joel would ring his bell once to say 'Hello – I'm right behind you', twice for 'Slow down – you're a little too far ahead', and multiple times if he wanted me to stop.

The light was a soft yellow as the sun leaned against the passing afternoon like a sleepy cat. I looked at my odometer and saw that, despite the feeling of paralysis and pain, the miles were passing. Joel and I barely spoke, both focused on pedalling and watching the tarmac roll beneath our wheels. After a long stretch of silence, I began to sing. I sang loud and out of tune, brashly throwing out every jazz standard I could think of. The more pain that rang through me, the louder I sang. I sang so loudly and so badly that I started to laugh, and as I laughed I started to cry, and to stop the tears I started to sing.

And so it went until we reached Cottage Grove.

Hidden almost out of sight behind a tree was a wooden sign etched with the words 'Echo Hollow Lane'. This was where a man named Pete lived, who, according to the owners of the Axe and Fiddle Bar, was going to provide us with a room for the night. The paved road ended where the sign began, and a gravel path led us through an avenue of tall trees.

I stood off my bike, removed my helmet and hung it on the handlebars. The stones crunched beneath the cleats on my shoes and slid beneath Joel's slowly rotating wheels beside me. In a few metres the main road was out of sight.

Golden light poured through the trees like paint swirling in a jar of clear water, igniting acid-green lichen that dripped off the heavy branches. The world glistened with a vividness that I'd never known before. I stopped walking and held my breath. I wanted to hear the sound of the light. It was clear that we were in an enchanted place.

A few metres further along we arrived at a clearing and a small dwelling. At first it appeared that no one was home, then a door swung open and we were greeted by an ageless man, his hair dark, his feet bare and his eyes glistening.

'Hey! You must be Jo. Welcome. I'm Pete. You just missed everyone. Had a big party last night. We were just swimming off the hangovers,' he said nonchalantly.

'Where did you all swim?' I asked.

'In the pond, just up there.' He pointed towards a thick grove of trees further along the path. 'You can camp up there, if you'd like.'

I felt my shoulders relax. We were home.

We leaned our laden bikes against a pile of timber in the shed and, still in our cycling clothes, wandered in the direction of the pond. Soon the path opened up, revealing a crystalline body of water surrounded by ancient trees and silence. The sky and the trees reflected upon its dark-green, mirror-like surface, magnifying the depth of the water. Pond-skaters skimmed across the surface, and, in the grasses along the edge, a hundred blinking eyes of newts and frogs sparkled.

'Joel, don't look,' I called. 'I'm going skinny dipping!'

He dutifully turned around and I peeled off my cycling clothes and entered the water. The ground beneath my feet was soft and otherworldly, the unfamiliar terroir oozing cold and grainy through my toes. The water kissed my skin, cold and kind, lapping against my inflamed muscles. Goosebumps crawled over my body, and the hairs on my arms quivered.

The smell of green grass rose upwards, and my eyes felt as if they, too, were turning as green as everything around me. I moved slowly, barely stirring the placid water. I had time and I was learning how to use it. The sun cast slivers of warmth through the trees onto my face. I closed my eyes and smiled, lifting my feet and sinking beneath the surface and into another world.

From under the black-green opaqueness, light came from a single source. Everything below me was unfathomably dark, like a pool of molasses, and near the surface a ghostly light glowed. The fresh water didn't sting my open eyes as I swam through the green. I had become green. The deeper I reached, the darker my skin became, until it was black-green like seaweed.

Coming back to the surface, I kept half of my face submerged and, like the frogs and newts, navigated the pond with only my eyes above the water. Every hair on my body danced as I moved through this new world.

My nipples, belly-button and every other part of me tingled with liberty. My neck numbed and relaxed with the cold. The only sounds filling my ears were the evening birdsong and the swish of water. I would have stayed in the pond forever, were it not for our show that night at the Axe and Fiddle.

We were welcomed by the owner of the Axe and Fiddle and directed to the stage, where we met our quintessentially grumpy sound guy. There was a small scattering of people in the crowd, providing just enough human energy to latch on to. We played one long set of original songs, our sparse band made up of ukulele, voice and double bass meaning it was a stretch for me to maintain momentum and fill the time we were allocated. After more than an hour of music-making, a drunken man called out, 'Sing us another one, honey,' his robust stomach about to burst another button on his plaid shirt, his white beard flecked with beer foam.

Joel and I didn't have to deliberate long about whether to do a second set. The room was now empty but for five people: three were semi-conscious on the bar, and the other two were heckling for songs and my phone number. But I embraced the scene, elated that we had got here by the sheer power of our bicycles, and as I sang I drowned out the cries, recalling the humming of the road.

The next morning I woke with my face pressed against the dewy-damp canvas of the tent. I had put my earplugs in to guard my dreams from the sound of Joel's snoring. We slept back to back, as a brother and sister might, any sexual tension now vanquished. I was relieved. As I took my earplugs out, the dawn revealed itself in a cacophony of birdsong. I was glad Joel was still asleep; I wanted to greet the day alone.

Carefully, one tooth at a time, I unzipped the tent just enough to fit myself through and slipped out into the day. My bare feet met the long wet grass, and there, glistening like an untold secret, was the pond. I left my clothes in the grass and dived in, undeniably waking every sense. Through bubbles and silt, I said, 'Good morning,' and watched as the world rippled into wakefulness around me.

By 8 a.m. Joel and I had packed up and ridden down the enchanted Echo Hollow Lane, and back onto the paved road of the comparably ordinary. Joel was intent on getting coffee before we biked out of Cottage Grove, so we pedalled a little out of our way to find a diner. I was getting impatient with this relaxed pace. In my mind, every day needed to start early so that we could end early and enjoy the afternoon and evening hours at our destination. I was yearning for solitude and independence and, in spite of the pain in my neck and shoulders, I was frustrated with our slowish pace. It wasn't until 9.30 a.m. that we finally left Cottage Grove, heading west towards the coast at last.

The GPS, set on 'bike', led us to a fire road on which no cars were allowed to drive. It sounded like a dream: 15 kilometres of car-free biking. We had been warned by locals at the show the night before that it was steep, but we weren't fazed by the idea of some hills. The fire road, however, was not only car-less, but tarmac-less, signless and merciless. The path was thick with dark, heavy gravel, and our wheels slipped with each turn of the pedals. I put my bike into granny gear, but I kept skidding and sliding, my wheels rotating only every other pedal-rotation. Joel biked ahead and I sank deeper into thoughts of giving up.

Less than a kilometre up the hill, I stopped and watched as Joel disappeared over what appeared to be a crest. *Why is this so easy for him?* I asked myself. *He doesn't seem to be worried at all. He's just along for the ride, and his journey ends in a few days anyway.* I was beginning to resent Joel, and irrationally felt that he was taking away from my achievements and goals for this journey because I was finding it so difficult when he, apparently, wasn't.

'Fuck...I can't, I can't, I can't, I can't,' I whispered as I held my aching head low over my handlebars, hot tears running down my nose. I was crumpling like a child against the pressure I had created for myself, and I was angry. Angry that I was failing and Joel wasn't. Angry that my neck hurt so much and there was nothing I could do about it. Ultimately, there was nothing I could do about any of it, so I got off the bike, dug my toes into the gravel, leant my shoulder against my handlebars and, bending deep into the weight of my bike, pushed uphill.

At that moment a woman in her late fifties came bounding down the hill in lightweight running shoes, her grey curly hair bouncing as she went. She stopped for a moment, jogging on the spot, and said with a smile, 'You're almost there – only a mile to the top.'

'Really? Oh, that's great,' I replied, suddenly hopeful. 'Does the paving start there as well?'

'Oh, no, not for another ten miles or so,' she said, her fixed smile suddenly seeming to mock me, though I knew she was only trying to help. Sixteen more kilometres of gravel. I had to find a way to befriend this nightmare.

I finally caught up with Joel to tell him the news. He wasn't much happier about it than I was, our blood-sugar levels at rock bottom. As the fog settled on our shoulders, we felt heavy and tired. Finally we crested the hill.

'I'll see you at the bottom,' I told him. 'You go ahead, because I'm going to be slow.'

I stood up on my pedals and started the long, slithery descent. At first I kept my fingers wrapped around my brakes like an octopus asphyxiating its prey, but when I realised I wasn't going to slip and fall, I started to enjoy the ride. With gravity doing most of the work, the kilometres started to fly by. The clouds lifted, and there, not 50 metres away, I saw the beginning of the new road. After the hours of insatiable crunching, growling and scraping, my wheels seemed to float on the tarmac, humming peacefully. Our spirits lifted and we biked on through the fields, chatting happily all the way.

The plan was to reach Elkton and go to Arlene's Diner for lunch. By the time we reached Elkton, though, all positivity had been wiped from my spirit once more. Joel left me in a puddle of tears and went to eat lunch, while I, letting my inner child out to have a tantrum in broad daylight, hoped he'd bring me back a root beer and a slice of pie. I still did not understand how dramatically my metabolism affected my mood and my ability to see things clearly. As soon as I ate, I felt better.

We soldiered on, now beginning to enjoy the biking, understanding that we had just overcome what might be the hardest climb we were going to face.

We slid into Reedsport at dusk, the magic hour settling on everything around us. Every flower, tree and blade of grass ignited in the gloaming. A herd of female elk ran like ballerinas through the field to our left, followed in hot pursuit by a smaller herd of males, which chased them back into the woods again. To our right, the Umpqua River rolled along in sapphire-blue ribbons.

My frustrations at our late start were long forgotten.

Relishing what was to become my favourite time of each day, we arrived in Reedsport more energised than we had been all day – just in time to enjoy a luxurious sleep in a hotel.

7

THERE BE WHALES

REEDSPORT – BANDON – BROOKINGS: 220 KILOMETRES

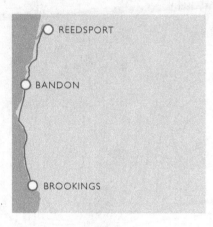

I woke up pain-free and therefore extremely happy. It was as though my body and mind had finally succumbed to the inevitability of the journey ahead and stopped complaining so much. We had arrived the night before just as dark was setting in, and hadn't noticed the sign on the corner of the road that said: 'Pacific Coast Highway'. We had made it to the road of my dreams. After almost 400 kilometres of the Great Song Cycle, I was elated to finally be on Highway 1. I punched the air with my gloved fist and hugged Joel, balancing my heavy bike awkwardly between my legs.

I took the lead. We had reached the Yellow Brick Road and were on our way to something extraordinary. We stopped in Winchester Bay, just a few kilometres down the road, to get breakfast.

When we pulled into the parking lot of a supermarket, a sky-blue Vespa approached us, its paintwork lined with

Illustration by Joanna Wallfisch

rust, its engine coughing like a lifelong smoker. Perched like a budgerigar upon a worn leather seat, wearing a helmet, flip-flops and a shell-suit with no shirt, was a man, his skin creased and orange. He stopped and stared hard at us with aquamarine eyes.

'There be whales out there,' he shouted in a voice as thick as tar, pointing beyond the supermarket. 'Whales, lots of 'em. Go. Go see. Go see them now. Before it's too late.'

He held our gaze and kept pointing, his hand stabbing at the air as if he were trying to turn on a broken television. We thanked him and followed his instruction. He was right – in the near distance we saw plumes of water bursting from the spouts of humpback whales.

The day passed easily. We were full of new energy: my body felt strong, my neck had recovered, and we ate regularly throughout the day, and so didn't have to face any foul moods or short tempers. We arrived in Bandon in the afternoon, and I called Susie, our next Warm Showers host, to let her know we were near.

'If I were you,' she told me, 'I'd go get some homemade ice cream, and then make your way here before the sun goes down so we can go for a swim in the lake.' Her voice was a complex marbling of innocent girl and wise woman.

Making our way down an unmarked lane that was carpeted with fallen bark and well-trodden gravel, we kept our eyes peeled for a red letterbox hidden in the trees. After a few doubtful circles we saw it, as Susie had described: a small wooden letterbox, tucked behind a bush, as if in a Beatrix Potter illustration. I felt like Alice in Wonderland as we were directed, as if by an unseen hand, down a path to a magnificent cedar home. There was nobody around so we found what looked like the front door, timidly climbed the rough-hewn wooden steps, and I knocked on the glass.

The door opened on its own and shyly I called out, 'Hello?'

Just then, with smiles abounding, Susie appeared and greeted us with open arms. 'Great, you're just in time. The fog is going to creep in soon. Let's go for a swim.'

Her home was in a grove of trees on the edge of an endless lake, its surface the black of a cat's eye, speckled with green lily pads. She handed us large towels and we trotted down to the small wooden jetty at the bottom of her garden.

'Watch your step – there might be splinters,' she called after me, but I was already skipping along the jetty, bursting with the glee of a child at their own birthday party. I stood at the edge of the jetty and stared into the water. It stared back at me, prehistoric and faceless as its depth absorbed all light. Only a sliver of a silvery sheen glimmered across the surface like a satin sheet, as it conversed with the white clouds above.

I knelt down and reached in with my hand, stroking the silken water like the scales of a dragon. I wanted to make friends with this organism, this beast, this beauty, this unknown. Just then the wooden slats on the jetty shifted as Susie and Joel arrived.

'This is your lake?' I asked Susie, amazed.

'Yes – well, sort of. I own part of it. I learnt to swim in this lake. My mother took us here as children, and I always knew I wanted to live here one day, so my husband and I built the house.'

Leaping off the jetty, my arms above my head, my toes pointed, I pierced the surface and let myself sink deep into its embrace. I fell through the water until I sensed the temperature drop around my toes, and I felt a chill run through me as if in warning. With one downward push of my arms I sent my body gliding back up to the glowing surface.

Susie and Joel were still chatting on the jetty, and so for a minute I was completely alone in this great lake. I turned to lie on my back, and I floated – legs and arms open, lungs full – and stared up at the open sky.

Susie and her husband were wonderful hosts. Joel and I were given our own rooms, and again I excused myself long before the sun had gone down. The solitude I found in sleep was precious to me.

In the early morning, after another glorious swim, we gathered our freshly laundered clothes. Pulling on my skin-clinging spandex was like putting on a coat of armour, all my bits and pieces held fast against my body with shining and brightly coloured elasticated fabric from breast to knee. Cinching my velcro straps tight across my foot and clipping into my pedals was like stepping into the stirrups hanging from the saddle of a patient stallion. My helmet, my sunglasses, my gloves. A ritual donning began to evolve. I felt empowered by my clothing, and by my trusty steed, which I knew would take me wherever I wanted to go.

The sun was warm and the world brilliantly scented with cedar, pine and wildflowers on the evaporating dew. We were excited about conquering our greatest daily distance yet, all the way to Brookings, where we were to meet a very old friend of mine, Edwin.

We had the wind on our backs, and the first 30 kilometres were flat and easy going. Ahead of us lay our first encounter with the ancient coastal redwood forests, and we biked with purpose towards them. As we approached Humbug

Mountain State Park, the road was sucked into the forest and away from the coast, and we were met with the majesty of the redwood trees. Our bikes tilted up with the incline of the road, towards the height of the trees. Endlessly upward we climbed for an unrelenting hour, stopping every few kilometres for water and a Clif Bar.

The climb encouraged me to meditate on every rotation of my wheels, feeling the chain whirring and turning, resisting gravity, driving me forwards, slowly, surely, happily. My heart raced as endorphins pumped through me. Sweat dripped ticklishly down the tip of my nose, and between breaths I licked it off with my tongue. My lungs burned as I stretched them with every deep gulp of air. Cars passed by abrasively, their aluminium shells skimming close to our soft skin; they knew nothing of the incline of this road.

I stood on my pedals and heaved my handlebars from side to side, pulling upwards as the weight of my luggage pulled me back. I threw my body weight forward and up, lifting my shoes, straining my knees, pointing my toes, breathing deeply into the hill, muscles burning and alive. I got into a rhythm and started to dance with my bike, with the hill, with the sunlight. I was so happy. We reached the top, had a drink and a long stretch. Preferring the climb to the descent, I let Joel go ahead.

The downward roll was swift, and soon we were back at sea level, ecstatic. We had lunch at Gold Beach and prepared for our next big climb, through Cape Sebastian State Scenic Corridor. The Oregon Coast Highway rolled towards the coastline and away, crossing the river and diving into the forest once more. The climb through Cape Sebastian was like a roller-coaster. As the road ascended, the redwoods grew in height, while their roots dropped downward below the steep banks of the hill. Soon it was impossible to see where the trees began and where they ended. I put my bike into granny gear and bore down into my saddle, keeping my cadence consistent, and looked around me in awe.

Each tree, with its unique fleshy bark, soft and splintering, folded like velvet, coated with lichen, glistening amber in the sunlight that filtered through the thick canopy, seemed to speak to me. It was like they were growing out of a bottomless canyon, their secrets forever hidden from view. Through heavy breaths, I talked to them, thanking them for allowing me into their home.

The climb continued for almost two hours. We were tired, and our morale was starting to fray. After eating yet another cardboard energy bar, we made it to the top. There the world opened up. We were out of the trees and above the clouds. We looked around at this new vision: soft, rolling clouds that stretched as far as the eye could see, the tips of the redwoods only just piercing through, like a miniature forest. Just before the road tilted downward to the descent, a traffic warden was organising the flow of the vehicles. There had been an endless and relentless stream of cars, trucks and RVs on the way up, a tiresome presence during the climb.

We weaved our way to the front of the queue and waited as the traffic warden turned her sign to STOP, said something into her radio, then winked at us. 'You guys go ahead – I'll hold the cars back for you,' she said. Such generosity and power wielded in that orange stop sign.

'Thank you,' we said in unison, and I blew a kiss to the cars as they bit our dust for once. As soon as we tipped over the crest of the hill, gravity took hold and we flew down the open road. Not a single car passed us in either direction. As well as stopping the traffic travelling down the hill, she had evidently radioed down to stop the traffic coming up as well. The road was our own, and we laughed and called out in happiness.

Joel soon disappeared at incredible speed around the bend, while I kept my pace a little more modest. My confidence rising, I released my brakes and stood on my pedals, holding my legs strong, knees bent and my body low over my bike. The weight of my panniers glued my wheels to the road, and I swooped downhill gracefully at 60 kilometres per hour, leaning into the corners, my eyes fixed on the furthest point. My mouth was dry, open against the wind in a perpetual grin. Tears rushed from my eyes and into my ears as the wind swept under my sunglasses.

My mind was completely quiet. All I could hear was the whooshing of air past my ears and the low humming of my wheels on the road. I was suspended between intense fear and immense joy, and I watched as my speedometer crept higher and higher. I had never known speed like this.

Up ahead, the road levelled for a moment before lifting for a brief ascent. I wanted to maintain my sensation of flight, so I sat and started to pedal as fast as I could. As soon as I spun the pedals I heard a snap. At first I thought I had ridden over a twig, as the sound was so strange, but the sensation of fire that roared up through my kneecap, up my thigh and down my shin told me otherwise. I winced as the pain took my breath away, and free-wheeled for a moment before gingerly pedalling again. I quickly realised that I couldn't put any strain through my left leg, so I pushed only with my right, my SPD shoe taking the strain.

Very soon the road straightened out, and in the near distance I could see the ocean again. I was too happy to worry about my knee: I was going to enjoy this ride and figure the rest out later. Leaning low over my handlebars once more, but staying in the saddle this time, I sped like a torpedo to the shoreline below. Knowing that I couldn't pedal, I free-wheeled, fingers off the brakes, and let my bike come to a natural stop.

Joel was just ahead, and I waved, grinning from ear to ear, as I slowed from 60 kilometres per hour to a stop in moments.

'Can you believe what we just did?' he gasped, more from excitement than from exertion. We looked up the road we had just descended, and saw the cars finally appear. We waved as they passed us by.

The rest of the afternoon was slow going. We were both tired, and my knee was definitely not right. Yet we had both clicked into a new gear, both physically and emotionally, after the trials of the first few days. Even though today had been our longest and hardest day so far, we were happy.

I was also looking forward to staying with old friends tonight, Bob and Edwin. My friendship with them harked back to childhood summers I'd spent with my mum in Carmel-by-the-Sea, California, where she'd directed the orchestra for the Carmel Bach Festival. Bob was a board member of the festival: white hair, gold teeth, sensible shoes. Edwin was a violinist, and somewhat of a Pied Piper, with his boundless energy and enthusiasm for playing his violin at every opportunity, whether on a stage or on the beach serenading the otters.

On the brink of collapse, Joel and I arrived at Bob's vacation apartment in Brookings. Edwin had been staying with Bob for a couple of days and greeted us at the gate, his beaming smile and freckles sparkling beneath wild curls of red hair waving atop his six-foot-eleven frame. Bob, who I had not seen since my early teens, took a few moments to adjust to Jo-the-adult, and finally handed me a cold beer.

For Joel and me, relief and pleasure at having arrived overrode most of our exhaustion. With Edwin, we each took a second can of beer and went down to the beach below the house. I was hobbling and could barely make my way down the twenty steps, so I hopped on my right leg, looking ahead at the promise of the Prussian-blue Pacific Ocean.

We stuck our beers in the sand and ran, walked and limped into the freezing Oregon water. It was so cold that it burned, and the three of us yelped and screamed with aliveness. Edwin was the first to dive in headfirst with a great splash. I followed suit, then Joel. The cold whisked the air from my lungs like a burst balloon. We laughed until our ribs hurt. The happiness we felt had no words.

8

THE ESCAPEE

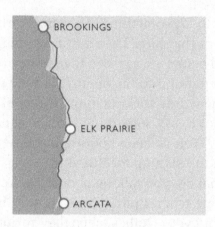

We left the majority of our luggage with Bob and Edwin. They would be driving through Arcata the next morning, on their way down to Carmel, so I arranged with our next hosts – the Sanctuary Art House in Arcata, where we would be in two days – to keep our bags safe until we arrived.

My knee was causing me a world of pain, but carrying 20 kilograms less on my bike made cycling more fathomable. Before leaving Brookings we stopped at a chemist to stock up on reams of bandage and a large bottle of Aleve. I was feeling very anxious about my knee. I'd just started to get into a strong rhythm, and now I had this setback. Joel, apparently, was doing just fine, with no physical issues and seemingly no emotional weight connected with the journey. He would be leaving tomorrow, and flying back home to New York. For him this was all fun; for me it was a mission, at which I would either succeed or fail.

I wrapped my knee with a bright-pink bandage and we rode, slowly, out of Brookings. Just a few miles down the road, I pulled over, on the brink of tears. I waved for Joel to pull over as well.

'I just want to say something,' I began. 'I've been chewing on a few things that have been getting to me over the last few days, and before we say goodbye tomorrow I think it's best to get them out into the open.' My tone was taut, and I could feel the words sticking in my throat like dry bread.

'Well, I want to say something too,' he shot back before I could go on. 'You've been nothing but miserable the last few days. I didn't sign up for this shit!'

'What? What are you talking about? You're the one who doesn't help me when I put all our laundry in the wash – you just take out your clothes when they're done. You make me navigate every day, you—'

'I make you navigate?' Joel broke in, astounded. 'Jo, if I even so much as *suggested* taking the lead, you'd bite my head off and remind me that this is your journey.'

'Well, this is really important to me. This isn't just fun, or a holiday. This is work for me – this is my album release tour. And I still have a thousand miles to go.' Tears were perched on my lower eyelids.

'Why are we even arguing right now?' Joel said, still shouting.

'Because I'm pissed off, and I want to know that you know how much this trip means to me.' The rationality of my thinking was diminishing with every sentence, and I felt small as I let this wave of negativity engulf me. 'Plus,' I continued, trying to stand my ground and find sense in my upset, 'my fucking knee hurts like hell, and I'm scared

that I won't be able to finish what I have set out to do.'
At this admission, the tears tumbled down my hot cheeks.

'I'm sorry, Jo,' Joel said, backing down. 'I just want to be
your friend, and I'm really grateful to be on this journey
with you.' He put a gentle hand on my shoulder. 'But I
really didn't sign up for arguing on the road like this.'

'Hey, I told you on our first meeting in the park that
I would get grumpy, that it wasn't going to be all roses,'
I reminded him.

'It's true, you did,' he admitted. 'I guess we just don't
know each other that well, do we?'

We had reached an equal footing. It was true we didn't
know each other well, yet in the space of just a few days
we had been through more trials and triumphs than most
lifelong friends. We hugged awkwardly, our bikes almost
falling to the ground, and then continued on towards
California.

Within the hour we reached the blue sign we had been
waiting for: 'Welcome to California'. Painted yellow
poppies reiterated the warmth of the greeting. Never
before had I found road signs to hold such significance, but
this landmark was momentous. As cars whizzed by us and
across the invisible boarder between one state and another,
we took a photo, touched the impervious structure and
rolled into California.

There was a palpable tempo shift on the road. It widened
and the traffic flow grew fast and loud. The cars seemed to
be in a rush, as if they were speeding towards the time of
their lives, hippies on a mission to a spiritual awakening

that only California could provide. As a consolation, the shoulder was wide and felt secure, with almost 6 feet between us and the cars.

We were 5 kilometres north of Crescent City, riding side by side and chatting easily, when we saw it.

'Oh, look, someone on a recumbent bike,' I said, pointing towards a dark blob far ahead. 'Man, they're riding really close to the edge of the shoulder.'

'Yeah, crazy. I'd never want to ride a bike that low to the road,' Joel responded lightly. 'Must be kind of scary. I hear they're super aerodynamic, though.'

'Whoa! What the hell are they doing?' I exclaimed as the recumbent veered over the white line of the shoulder and into the stream of traffic. It then appeared to throw a 360 before slithering back to the relative safety of the shoulder.

We looked at each other, confused. Something wasn't right about this. As the distance between us closed, we began to understand the reality of what we were seeing.

'Wait – that's not a recumbent bike, that's a wheelchair. There's someone in a wheelchair on the highway,' I said, gasping, and then we both let out a laugh of disquiet.

'Maybe they're doing some kind of ride for charity?' Joel asked, uncomfortably optimistic. 'They're moving so fast, they must be pretty strong. I bet it's some young dude pulling a crazy prank or something.'

We were still too far away to distinguish any of the occupant's features, except for what looked like a grey wig perched on top of their head. Then, all of a sudden, the chair spun 180 degrees, rolling backwards in zigzags into the oncoming flow of traffic, and faced us. For a split second our eyes met with two dark, inconsolable holes buried in the deep creases of a old woman's face, all lines and anger. Before spinning around again, she waved her two canes in the air like a pirate declaring war. Then, placing one cane on the road, she deftly spun back around and continued on.

Joel and I were now barely 15 metres behind her, so we slowed our pace, trying not to get too close. Every few moments she would spin her chair by kicking off the road with her slippered feet, and take a leap of faith into the traffic again. We started waving the cars down, directing them to change lanes and give this kamikaze pensioner room to perform her deadly ballet on wheels.

'We have to call the police,' I said to Joel. 'This is crazy. I really don't want to see someone die today.'

He agreed without hesitation, and dialled 911. The operator put us through to highway patrol and Joel explained the situation. 'There's an old woman riding down the highway in her wheelchair, and she keeps throwing 360s into the oncoming traffic. Maybe she's escaping from a local retirement home? Come quick – we think she's on a suicide mission.'

A highway patrol car appeared minutes later. The driver had kept his sirens off, and I appreciated his discernment of the situation by not startling the woman into doing something even more impetuous. He slowed as he passed us, and we waved him forward to where she was rolling along.

She seemed oblivious to the patrol car's presence until he was beside her and bleeped his siren once. She whipped her chair around but did not stop. Instead, she put both her canes into the road and started pushing faster than ever, with the motion of a cross-country skier. We were right behind her now and could hear her screaming expletives as the policeman finally managed to stop her in her tracks.

There was nothing more we could do. As we passed the unlikely pair, the old lady stopped screaming at the

policeman and turned to give us the finger. She held our
gaze, her downturned mouth a valley of frowns, the middle
finger of one hand steady, her cane beating the air furiously
with the other.

Later in the afternoon, the road opened up and we passed
majestic swathes of redwoods. A symbiosis was emerging
with every rotation of our pedals, forming a bond between
road, wheels, body, breath, mind, thoughts, vision, sky, air,
light, silence, noise, pain and elation. As we approached
Prairie Creek Redwoods State Park, the road extended in
a long, straight descent, the yellow traffic lines converging
towards a vanishing point that kept disappearing, no
matter how fast we flew down the hill.

'Look where we are!' I called out to Joel, sure we had
woken in the middle of a glorious dream.

The mouth of the forest lay ahead of us, agape with
wonder. As we entered the shadows of the trees, the magic
was palpable. Ancient faces surrounded us. Every trunk
had a different expression: smiling, singing, laughing,
frowning, crying, a metamorphosis of spirit and nature.
Each trunk was wider than any car, and that immense girth
stretched skyward to meet a canopy that seemed to kiss
the moon.

We had one final climb before the day was done, but the
air was cool, the light a silvery sheet that ignited the green
of the lichen and red of the bark, and there was little we
could complain about. It was dusk by the time we reached
Elk Prairie Campground. We found a pitch in the hiker-
biker site under an oak tree. There was a gaggle of other

cycle-tourists camping, and we spent the evening sharing stories and snacks with one another. One couple, Adam and Philippa, were nearing the end of their round-the-world bike trip. They were originally from London, and had spent the last year cycling through Europe, Australia and the Americas. My plan seemed pithy next to their triumphant route.

The moon was a bright orb that night, and sent a glow through the tent canvas that penetrated my dreams. In the early morning I limped out of the tent and went to brush my teeth and dress in the washrooms. Blocking the path between me and the toilets, two fully grown male elk were sparring, their antlers clacking arrhythmically, their hooves landing on the dewy ground with a thump. Other campers started to emerge, standing watchfully by their tents as we witnessed this great display of strength and grace.

I brushed my teeth with water from my bottle, peed in the long grass behind the tent and got dressed in the open. Joel and I biked out of the campground just as the sun rose over the mist-covered field, lighting the dew-dappled spiderwebs that were strung over the long grass like chandeliers.

Our combined moods slipped between the cracks of anticipation and enthusiasm for the day ahead, never quite settling on one or the other. We were digging deep for the energy required to reach Arcata, but also holding back to avoid the reality of Joel's imminent departure.

The ride to Arcata was relatively short, taking us swiftly from forest to ocean to urban bike path. We wanted to get there early so we could explore the town together and indulge in some Mexican food, but Joel had lost his wallet with his ID two days earlier, so he would have to go directly to the airport to make sure he could actually fly out the next morning.

For the final 15 kilometres I insisted we play 'Just a Minute', an old radio game show in which you have to speak on any subject for a full minute, without hesitation, repetition or deviation. Joel did not want to play. He wanted to ride that final hour in silence, with space to reflect on the last eight days. This was his last day on the road. I was not yet sensitive to the impact of this fact, and continued loudly, jostling him and selfishly trying to pass the time; all I wanted to do was arrive so that I could have two days off the bike again.

Everything went into fast-forward, and without warning we were crossing the bridge into Arcata. It was as though the curtain had dropped before the actors could take their bow. We arrived at the Sanctuary Art House, and found our bags, as promised, waiting for us in the hallway. Before we could share even a celebratory cup of tea, Joel rode his bike to the local bike shop to get it packed up and sent back to New York, and then took a taxi to the airport, while I waited back at the house. The cold practicality of it all was a bitter anticlimax, and we were both too numb and exhausted to acknowledge the emotion of the day.

I greeted our host, Sebastian – a young, skinny fellow with a light mop of blond hair and rake-like limbs, over which he draped an unbuttoned blue linen shirt and brown corduroy trousers. I showered and gradually unwound in the comfort of the artists' commune. Joel returned late, tired, hungry and sad. He would have to go to the airport as soon as it opened and, as the ticket officer had unhelpfully told him, just talk his way onto the flight. I helped him pack, and we went to sleep just before midnight. We shared the living-room floor, our final few hours in convivial company.

'I'm going to miss you,' I said quietly into the dark room.

'I'll miss you too,' he whispered.

'Thank you for coming with me this far. I don't think I could have done this ride without you,' I admitted.

'You're welcome,' he said. 'Thank you for having me along. This has been the best time of my whole life.'

We lay facing each other, curled up like worms in our sleeping bags, and closed our eyes. Joel had been my companion, my friend and, on so many occasions over the last 800 kilometres, my strength. He had waited patiently as I threw tantrums, cried into my root beer, pedalled off in frustration, told him where we would go, eat and sleep that night. He kept my spirits above rock bottom with bad jokes and good conversation. He was my wing mirror when I couldn't turn my head, and the social leader when I was too tired to talk to the people we met. He knew how much this trip meant to me and had done everything to enable it. As sleep descended, this realisation washed over me like a wave and I took his hand. I was really going to miss having him there.

Long before the sun rose, Joel crept out from his sleeping bag, already dressed, whispered goodbye and left. I watched him through the window as he got into a taxi and drove away into the pre-dawn. I returned to my sleeping bag, turned over and went back to sleep, alone for what felt like the first time.

9

SANCTUARY ART HOUSE

ARCATA – PEPPERWOOD: 68 KILOMETRES

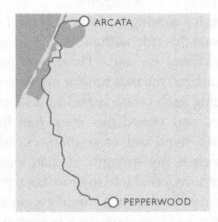

I sat at the end of the long, knotted wooden table in the kitchen, eating oats and fresh peaches, and scribbled in my journal. At the other end of the table were Sophie and John, a couple who lived in the small room behind the stage upstairs. They were nuzzling over a cookery book, their fingers exploring each other's hands and arms. Their noses were touching as they whispered to each other in their lovers' dialect, their tongues occasionally reaching out towards the other's, then slipping back like a lizard smelling the surroundings.

In the other room, Sebastian was playing a stride version of 'Mood Indigo' on the honky-tonk upright piano, the buttons on the cuffs of his long shirt sleeves occasionally clicking on the keys. Hannah, her straw-blond haircut asymmetrically to her chin, and her rosy mouth upturned in a coy smile, like a child who knows a secret, spun the sewing wheel, threading lines of satin and beads together for her next fairytale creation. The cupboards were bursting with home-dried fruits, sliced apples and pears, spices and herbs, and from the oven rose the heady smell of baking bread.

The garden was accessible through a small window, just big enough for a large dog; you had to climb a footstool and squeeze through. Outside was a hand-powered washing machine. I took all my clothes and scrubbed them with suds and cold water as the sun beat down on my tired shoulders. I hung my array of lightweight synthetic clothing on the line strung above the veggie patch, then wandered into downtown Arcata in search of a massage.

The sensation of walking was strange, and I felt like I was missing something; it seemed slow, impractical and clumsy. My bike was beginning to become an extension of my body. But my knee was happy for the alternative motion, and I walked mindfully down to the main street. I spent the next few hours wandering aimlessly, browsing stores that sold healing crystals and colourful wall hangings, and organic cafes serving superfood smoothies and salads. Passing a music store, I noticed a poster in the window advertising a cellist who was also touring by bike. Turns out I was not the only one to come up with this idea.

When I returned to the Art House it had been transformed for the evening's Art Walk and my concert. Hannah's creation decorated the front door and patio: a silken tent with a floor cushion, and instructions next to a pad of paper: *Write your thoughts and put them in the box.*

The whole house was an array of eclectic creations; in the main room whimsical wood cuttings of animals hung on the walls. The stage was set and the empty pews held the promise of a hundred new friends to share my music with. By six o'clock the house was full of people of all ages, milling around on every floor, following the art trail curated by the resident and local artists. The trail led back up to the main hall, where I would be performing. When everyone was congregated, it was my turn to present my art in the form of song.

In the front row sat a man in his sixties, his round face fixed in a perpetual smile. Over his rotund stomach stretched a bright-red T-shirt, and a thought occurred to me: *If Santa Claus was a stoner, maybe he'd be this guy.* As part of my show banter, I explained the details of my bike tour to the audience. I then mentioned that I was heading for Leggett tomorrow – it was 160 kilometres away, which would make it the longest day of the tour so far. I also slipped in that my knee was bothering me rather a lot, hoping that some group sympathy would help it heal overnight.

After the show, my green-eyed Santa Claus approached me and said, 'I'm driving to Pepperwood tomorrow, and I'd be happy to give you a ride.' He took my hand in his padded palm and shook it, introducing himself. 'I'm Steve. Loved your show, by the way!'

My heart simultaneously leapt and sank. He was offering me an escape route: Pepperwood was almost halfway to Leggett, which would save me almost 70 kilometres on the bike. It would be cheating, but it was also an opportunity for me to continue my journey despite my knee injury.

Steve scrawled his phone number on the back of a page he tore from a *Men's Health* magazine and told me to call him that night – 'no matter how late' – and let him know if he should pick me up in the morning.

The house was quiet once more. I busily repacked my panniers, folding everything immaculately, trying to find space for each item, imagining that I could somehow lighten the load just by placing things more neatly. I packed and repacked until finally I resolved to just get the bags closed and onto my bike.

My mind was full of noise. I really did not want to accept the offer of a ride in the morning, but I couldn't keep denying that my knee was in bad shape. I called three of my closest friends back home and asked them if they thought I would be a failure if I accepted the ride. Of course, every one of them had the same response: 'Take the ride. Enjoy it!' Malinda, my neighbour in Brooklyn – and a professional masseuse – tipped my decision by telling me straight: 'If you don't take a break now, you might have to give up on your whole trip. Don't mess around with knees!'

Steve picked up after the first ring. He seemed happy to hear from me, and we arranged to meet just before 8 a.m. When I put the phone down I sighed and sat alone at the wooden table, fat tears pooling on the knotted surface and rivering through the cracks.

The house was still asleep when I left in the morning, and on the kitchen table I left a note of thanks. I wheeled my bike out through the basement, where it had been resting for the last two days, past potting wheels, towers of drying apples, jars of homemade preserves, boxes of tools and leaning canvases. I bade this unique place adieu with a curtsy and went out into the gentle morning.

Steve was late, and for a while I pictured getting on my bike and cycling all the way to Leggett after all. Just as I had resolved to do this, his red Volvo appeared around the bend. I would have to relinquish my desire to know every kilometre of the road ahead. We struggled to get my bike into the trunk, in the end removing both wheels and twisting the handlebars around so it was almost flat against itself. I felt a surge of guilt, as though I were betraying it, and whispered to the frame, 'I'm sorry – you'll be out soon.'

As we drove out of Arcata, I watched in the wing mirror as the pretty town disappeared and was almost immediately replaced by a grim and soulless no man's land of strip malls, factory outlets and gas stations. I was all of a sudden not so sad to be missing out on these particular kilometres. Even so, I stared out the window, trying to imagine how the road would have felt rumbling through my body if I were on my bike.

We took a small detour to the post office. After the two days biking from Brookings to Arcata with half of my luggage, it was clear to me that I was simply carrying surplus weight. My next show wasn't until Oakland, in San Francisco, in almost a week's time, so I decided to FedEx some things there. Into a large box I placed my loop pedal, two dresses, a pair of leggings, my running shoes and twelve Clif Bars. It was exciting to send the box south, knowing that it would be waiting for me when I arrived – and knowing that when I arrived, I would have conquered the kilometres in between. This package was a carrot hanging in front of my nose.

Steve and I drove another 30 kilometres or so through concrete suburbia until finally, with a dramatic scene change from grey to green, we arrived at the Avenue of the Giants.

Through the open windows of the car I could smell the sweetness of the warming woods as the morning sun rose high and started to bake the earth. My gaze flickered back and forth from the glorious outside to the small blue dot on the car's GPS unit that marked where in the world we were.

'Are we there yet?' I asked Steve, anxious to get out and back on my bike.

'Almost, just another few bends.' he replied, though we continued driving for what felt like hours.

I held onto the door handle like a parachutist ready to jump. I wanted to get out, reassemble my poor bike and be on the road again, travelling solely under my own power. I was sure I was cheating, and my guilt swelled with every kilometre that passed. I bit my lip, leaned my head out of the window and closed my eyes against the tingle of my tear ducts. I didn't want to appear ungrateful.

At last Steve said, 'We're here.' He pulled up in a clearing. There was a single post with an arrow pointing into the forest and the words 'Hiking Trail'. I stepped out of the car, setting my bare feet on the dusty earth. The ground was warm and smelled sweet.

I hopped over the soft dirt to open the trunk. Steve helped me take my bike and luggage out of the car, and, trying not to get myself covered in grease, I put the wheels back on, tightened the rack and fixed my chain onto the cogs. I clicked all five of my bags into place: two on the back, two on the front and the handlebar bag. Sitting between my hands, in the bright-yellow box-bag, were 3 litres of water sloshing around in a CamelBak. When I'd strapped my ukulele case securely on top of the back rack, my shining steed was ready to go.

'You must be hungry?' Steve said in a kind, fatherly tone.

'I made you a tuna sandwich. You should eat it before you go.'

I accepted gladly, and he watched as I devoured the sandwich. Then it was time to say goodbye. Clipping into my pedals, I tested my left knee with a few gentle cycles. I turned to wave a last farewell to Steve, but he had already trundled off into the woods for his own adventure.

10

ALONE

PEPPERWOOD – GARBERVILLE – LEGGETT: 98 KILOMETRES

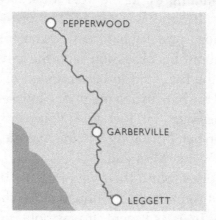

I looked back once more as I peddled along the empty road.
There was nobody around. I was alone for the first time on
this journey. The realisation of my solitude surged through
me like a wave, and I let out a whimper that immediately
fell silent on the pine-covered ground.

'Well, Jo, it's just you and me from now on. Here we
go,' I said, listening as my voice disappeared into the trees
without even so much as an echo. I rode forward slowly, the
silence around me broken only by the hum of my wheels
and the birdsong hidden deep in the endless forest. I had
been yearning for solitude since the start of the ride; now
that I had it, I wasn't so sure I wanted it after all.

Above the whirring of my wheels I heard my stomach
rumble. The tuna sandwich Steve had given me had already
been engulfed by my increased metabolism. I'd lost all track
of time, cycling pensively and in awe of the magnificent

trees, and had ignored the kilometres gathering on my odometer. Almost an hour had passed, yet I'd seen not one car.

I pulled over and opened my handlebar bag to see a protein bar smiling up at me. Joel must have snuck it in before he left. It was the last of his favourite kind: a mint-choc-chip mega-protein bar, with extra protein. I had teased him about his obsession with these bars but now I was glad of the fuel, and to be reminded of his company. I unwrapped the bar, turned my phone into selfie mode and sent Joel a message: 'Hi, Joel, wish you were here. Thanks for the protein bar. I'm eating it in the Avenue of the Giants, and it's bloody hot. Miss you.'

As the calories found their way into my bloodstream, I began to feel brighter and continued along the silken road, talking to the trees as I went. It was hot. Hotter than hot. Heat permeated from every direction beneath the shade of the trees, from the black tarmac below to the shadows of the canopy above. I was riding through a convection oven. Thankfully, my forward motion created a cooling breeze, but whenever I stopped to stretch or have a snack the heat wrapped around me like a blanket. Sweat poured down my face and into my eyes, and down my back, my shins and into my socks. My body felt like a tropical rainforest.

I came to a small town in the middle of the Avenue of the Giants, which consisted of a handful of cabins and a hotel. I had been drinking constantly, and my two water bottles and 3-litre CamelBak were empty, with only dregs of warm water left in the bottom. A few metres ahead, an older gentleman was watering the plants outside of Myers Inn, spreading cold water over the foliage as if the word 'drought' didn't exist. I pulled up beside him, leaned my bike against the fence and asked if I might have some water. He looked me up and down, taking in my beetroot-red complexion, sweat-drenched hair and cheerful smile, and handed me the hose. I lifted it above my head and stood beneath the cooling stream until every inch of me was saturated and renewed. The old man waited patiently until I was done. He didn't say a word, but in his eyes was a twinkle of amusement. While I still had the hose, I filled up my vessels with water, thanked him and continued on my way, my wet skin sparkling with the breeze.

I was starting to love the day – and being alone. The road itself was incredible, mostly flat and so smooth that riding was effortless, except for the need to sustain my energy through the heat of the day. By now it was almost noon, and as I passed by Hidden Springs Campground I spotted Philippa and Adam, the cycling couple I had met at Elk Prairie Campground three days earlier. I waved from the road and they beckoned me in to say hello. I rolled into the campground, happy to see familiar faces. San Francisco was their final destination, and, realising that they would get there long before they needed to if they biked every day, they had decided to camp out for a few nights, taking the final days of their journey easy. Adam announced he was about to go on a mission to get a bottle of wine, so after I'd had a brief catch-up with Philippa, he and I biked off together.

It was fun to have somebody to chat with again, even if for a short time. Time itself had begun to shift, and every minute felt enormous. We got to the store in the town of Miranda and, once he was armed with a bottle of red and I with an ice cream, we said goodbye.

It was over 40 degrees Celsius in the shade, and I was down to just 2 litres of water again. Just before 1 p.m. I reached the end of the Avenue of the Giants, and just like that I was unceremoniously spat out from the shelter of the forest and onto the shadowless, fast and furious Highway 101. I had spent the morning bathing in the magic that emanated from the forest, and now the sun was beating down like a flame-thrower. I couldn't drink enough. I crouched low over my handlebars and listened to my breathing.

I tried to talk out loud to find a semblance of balance and a sense of self, but only a garble of single words came out: 'Breathe. Pedal. Breath.' My awareness was dwindling as my body and mind struggled against the heat. Through the heat haze I had an idea, and pulled over on a verge to dig around in my pannier. I put on my long-sleeved windbreaker, poured water on my head and wrapped my light cotton scarf around my head and neck like a babushka. Placing my helmet over the scarf, I then created a turban of clothing on top of my helmet to create a barrier between the sun and my brain. In spite of the extra layers, I felt protected and microscopically cooler.

Before getting back on my bike I looked around to see if any drivers had noticed me there. I wanted to catch somebody's eye, if for a split second, and make a cry for help or just solidarity. But I was alone. I started pedalling along the shoulder again, my stark shadow casting an alien silhouette on the grey road.

Slowly my thoughts began to straighten out, and I concentrated on turning the pedals and winding down the kilometres until I could stop at the next major town and have a break. To the right of the highway was a large, fast-flowing river, its water acid-green. I longed to find a way to the river and jump in, but no roads led to its banks. Water,

water everywhere, but not a drop to quench this ever-mounting nightmare.

Breathe. Pedal. Breathe.

I stared at my front wheel as it turned over and over and over, concentrating on the blur of road passing beneath. I could hear my tires sticking to the road as the top layers of rubber melted on the asphalt.

Leggett was still over 60 kilometres away, and I was starting to doubt my ability to make it that far. If I could at least get to Garberville, I decided, I would stop there for the night. For now, however, I had no option to stop. I was in the middle of nowhere, crawling alone along the narrow shoulder of Highway 101 at 14 kilometres per hour.

Cars and RVs, their windows closed to keep the heat out, sped past me at 110 kilometres per hour, whisking up gritty air that pierced my eyes and stung my nostrils. Slowly but steadily pushing down on the pedals, I continued up endless hills, cresting false summits, reaching out towards mirage after mirage. As the temperature grew ever more unbearable, my only solace was that I was still moving, and therefore getting closer to the end of this ordeal.

Breathe. Pedal. Breathe.

By 3 p.m. I made it to Garberville. As I transitioned from the speed of the highway to the sleepy main street, my ears rang in the silence. I stopped at a quaint cafe called Flavours, almost falling sideways as I slowed my bike to a stop and tried to step off. The muscles in my legs and arms shivered with dehydration and exhaustion. I was struggling to coordinate my movements, even to see straight.

I propped my bike against the brick wall, then dropped heavily into one of the plastic chairs out front of the cafe. As soon as I was sitting still, I started panting like a dog. I couldn't slow my breathing or close my mouth to take in air through my nose. My tongue hung out as I panted, deep, heaving gasps, trying to cool down from the inside. As I sat there hyperventilating, panic rose in me. I put my head in my hands between my knees and began to cry, loudly and deeply. My stomach clenched in pain and my head throbbed between my gloves. I couldn't take a full breath. For the first time I was scared, and I was no longer able to contain it.

I tried to open my eyes but my eyelashes were glued together with tears and sweat. Through the blur I noticed a pair of bare feet. I looked up halfway and saw a man, his head cocked towards his bony shoulder, his fingernails blackened, his trousers held up with a length of rope. His weathered face hid his youth. 'Are you gonna be okay?' he inquired gently.

His voice was kind and something in his tone calmed me. For the first time in minutes I managed to inhale a full gulp of air, filling my lungs and slowing the dizziness. 'Yes, I think so,' I said quietly. 'Thank you.'

'Okay. Take care, now,' he said, and disappeared.

I slumped back in the chair, my sunburnt skin stinging on the plastic. My breath was still quivering but I knew I was going to be okay. I pushed myself up to standing and went inside the cafe.

The air-conditioning was on full blast and hit me like a bucket of ice. Deciding to ignore my vegetarian notions, I ordered a large turkey sandwich with extra Swiss cheese, a bag of potato chips, a large iced coffee and a cookie. While I was waiting for my food, I went to use the bathroom.

I sat down to pee but nothing came out. Not one drop of the 5 litres of fluid I had consumed that morning had reached my bladder.

I stood and looked in the mirror. Bloodshot eyes stared back at me through swollen, violet cheeks. The veins on my temples pulsed, and for a moment I hardly recognised myself.

After splashing cold water on my face, arms and chest, I walked back out to the cafe, taking a table by the window so I could watch my bike. My food was brought to my table by a skinny teenager wearing a tank top with a faded Metallica symbol on the front. I marvelled at the towering sandwich in front of me, held together with two toothpicks, yellow plastic frills only just peeking out from the sourdough. After carefully removing the toothpicks, I devoured the sandwich and potato chips, licked the salt that stuck to the inside of the foil packet, and ordered a second iced coffee. I also drank large cups of iced water, and filled my bottles again.

I spent more than an hour sitting in the window booth, the pleather seat sticking to my bare legs, and watched as the sleepy world of Garberville came and went. I absorbed the soundtrack of the cafe: the coffee machine grinding, the chef calling from the kitchen hatch, the bell on the door jingling as it opened and closed, letting in a bellow of hot air that was instantly rejected by the cold space, the abstract chatter of locals hanging at the counter sipping on milkshakes and chewing on dripping burgers. Slowly, I started to feel like me again.

The bell on the cafe door jingled. Behind the unwelcome heat strode a tall man, his gait wide, his black hair matted with old pomade, a neatly twisted goatee on his stubbled chin and silver rings on every finger. He stood in the doorway and took in the scene, then settled his green eyes on me. Without an invitation, he sat down opposite me, placing his elbows on the table. In a voice too bright for his roguish appearance, he asked, 'Is that your bike out there?'

Trying to find my words amid a rush of thoughts, I said, 'Yep.'

'Where are you headed today? You should stay here in Garberville.' His voice was rapid and enthusiastic.

'I'm going towards Leggett,' I replied vaguely.

'What's that strapped to the top of your bike? Is that an instrument or something?'

'Yeah, that's a ukulele. I'm on a kind of concert tour right now,' I admitted.

'No way! That's pretty rad.' His buoyancy was unrelenting. 'You should definitely stay here then – a couple of days, in fact. I work at that theatre over there.' He was pointing across the street to a semi-dilapidated, whitewashed building that had a large blue and red sign reaching up from the marquee: 'THEATER'. 'You could play on my radio show tonight, or tomorrow if you wanted. Maybe even do a set at the theatre.'

His effusive invitation was attractive, and I couldn't help but smile at his bravado. I considered my options awhile, knowing that time was as unrelenting as this stranger and I had to keep moving.

'Tell ya what,' he pushed, 'stay here and I'll drive you to where you gotta go tomorrow.' Then his phone rang. 'My ex!' he drawled, and rolled his eyes. He stood and walked out of the cafe, calling behind him, 'Don't go anywhere – I'll be right back.'

I watched as he ran across the hazy street and ducked through the ornate blue doors into the theatre.

Before he came back, I'd decided that I would make it to Leggett. Just as the hottest part of the day waned, I pedalled out of Garberville and back onto Highway 101.

Not 7 kilometres out of Garberville, the uncanny monotone voice of Siri spoke up over the roar of the traffic. 'In 600 feet turn right on Benbow Drive.'

I was surprised to hear this instruction and looked at the map. There was a small road running parallel to the highway, wending towards the river. It seemed there was a better cycling route than the relentless highway, and I was happy to follow it if it meant some respite from the cars, and possibly a swim in the river. As instructed, I took a right off the highway and bumped heavily down a poorly maintained road. I concentrated on balancing as I sped down the roughly hewn terrain. My bike jostled violently over the potholes and gravel, sending my luggage clanking against the rack. My bones vibrated with every bump, and my hands started cramping from clutching and pumping the brakes too hard. Dust flew up into my face as the sun beat down with vigour.

Finally the road levelled out and I came to a natural, if ungraceful, stop. I looked up and saw the highway stretching high above and out of reach, the sound of the traffic nothing but a rustle of autumn leaves. I had been concentrating so hard on not falling off that I hadn't noticed how far this road had strayed from the highway. Ahead of me was an open gate leading up a dirt track towards an abandoned campsite, its welcome sign fallen and leaning solemnly against its post. My skin rippled, and the hairs on my neck stood on end. My aloneness was absolute.

I looked back up the rough hill from where I had come, and then at the narrow, unpaved winding road ahead of me. I couldn't face getting back up that hill. I compared the map with the landscape and calculated that this road would offer me a good 10 kilometres of quiet riding. I ignored my best instincts and pushed down on my pedals, riding bumpily onward, through the open gate and past the thorny hedges that separated the road from the river.

My back wheel spun as I pedalled over dirt and sand, and I was so frustrated by the lack of traction that I didn't see the large pit bull terrier sleeping in the shade of a pickup truck until my front wheel was almost on top of it. There was nobody in the cabin, and seemingly nobody around either. The truck was strewn with dozens of animal bones, a morbid display decorating the dusty dashboard and filling the cargo space. Tied with string through its eye holes to the front grille, like the figurehead on a pirate ship, was a large sheep's skull, its horns twisted.

I looked hard at the dog: its muscular ribs rising and falling gently, it was in a deep sleep. I stopped breathing as my heart thumped through my chest, urging me to flee for my life, but the dog didn't seem to notice me – or if it did, it didn't care. I looked around once more to see if its owner might be near but there was no sign of life. Quietly I rolled past the dog and continued.

My heart was now racing, and all fatigue I had previously felt had been replaced by pure adrenaline. I pushed on the pedals as hard as I could, pulling up on my handlebars, trying to move my loaded bike faster than the meagre 10 kilometres per hour the terrain allowed. No matter how fast I pedalled, I could not increase my speed. Then I remembered the penknife in my handlebar bag. I found it buried beneath sunblock and protein bars and slipped it in my bra. The blade was barely 2 inches long, and it would take some fiddly manoeuvring to release it from its holder, but I felt marginally more secure knowing it was within reach.

For the next fifty minutes I put in the energy of a sprinter as I forged my way along this forsaken path. I knew that if I kept riding I would eventually return to the populated stream of the highway above. It was only a matter of time. I hardly acknowledged the picturesqueness of this road as it curved alongside the green river, my senses heightened beyond enjoyment, focusing instead on survival. Every few kilometres I would spy the tail of another pickup truck abandoned in the bushes, and my wheels would spin in the dirt as I urged myself away from this place, as though chased by an invisible force.

Getting my wheels back onto the paved highway was like waking from a bad dream. The indistinguishable energy that was pulling me backward relinquished its grasp.

The highway had been thrown into shadow as the sun dipped beneath the tips of the tall trees. In the flat light the road seemed vaster than ever, stretching endlessly to the north, from where I'd come, to the south, where I was trying to get to. Six lanes of cars hurtled forward in each direction, with only thin white lines separating them. The light was a pale pink, and the tarmac continued to reflect the morning's torment.

I climbed and climbed and climbed. Looking backwards down the highway, it seemed to stretch on forever, as if the more I pedalled, the more road there was. I was starting to feel desperate, on the verge of abandoning hope.

I pulled on my brakes, put both feet on the ground and considered my options. There was nowhere to sleep here, other than in the scrubby bushes which lined the highway. That was not an option. Turning back towards Garberville was not an option either. I had no choice: it was do or die. And I had no intention of dying, of lying down and being rolled into the tarmac's ever grumbling surface, so I just had to keep going. Somewhere inside me I had to find the will to keep turning the pedals for another 25 kilometres.

I could be in Leggett in an hour and a half, I told myself; I had heard there was a hiker-biker site in the Standish-Hickey Recreational Area, to the north of the city, and was hoping to make it there. I could make it before dark. I had to. I would get there, I would shower, I would eat, and I would sleep safely in my tent. It was only a matter of time.

I looked at the windows of the cars flying past me, and for a split second caught the eye of a young woman who had her bare feet propped up on the dashboard. She leaned forward as the vehicle passed and looked back at me, putting her hand against the closed window as if to say good luck. I lowered my eyelids till my eyes were half-closed, blurring the reality of the climb ahead, picturing nothing but the relief of my imminent arrival. Beyond that my task was simple. Breathe. Pedal. Breathe.

The road narrowed and tilted downward, with a steep camber at every turn. The air had finally relinquished its heat, and the sky turned a dusty blue as the night drew in. I turned on my headlight. Gift shops grinning with candy, postcards and sodas paraded along the side of the road. I was tempted to stop and browse but I didn't want to delay my arrival any further. Ten kilometres to Leggett.

The road grew narrower and windier, and the cars more aggressive, passing with only a layer of paint between them and me. The sky was darkening with every minute. Ahead I saw a sign: 'Redwoods River Resort and Pub, 0.5 miles'. It wasn't Leggett, but it would do. My body took over, and minutes later I swooped into the wide entrance of the resort. I had made it. Nine litres of water and two iced coffees and I hadn't peed all day, but I had made it.

REDWOOD

I carefully stepped off my bike, my legs numb with exhaustion, and walked towards the reception area. I leaned my bike against the timber door frame, peeled my helmet from my sweat-caked hair and put it under my arm. There were two kids in swimsuits buying popsicles, and when they saw me they ran out the door, giggling.

'Hi,' I croaked. 'Do you have any tent spots left for one night? I'm kind of desperate.' I was trying not to cry, my eyes welling up. 'I'll take anything,' I added before the lady behind the counter had time to respond. 'I just need somewhere to stay.' I was so tired.

She smiled, noticing my emotion, and took a quick look at her computer. 'Yep, you're in luck – we have one tent pitch left. It's the smallest one we have. It'll be thirty-five dollars.'

It was not the $5 hiker-biker rate I was used to, but nevertheless my shoulders dropped in relief. I placed my helmet on the counter so I could balance myself with both hands. 'Thank you,' I whispered as if in prayer – then I said it again, this time to her. I purchased the pitch, along with a root beer and an ice cream, both of which I had consumed in the time it took for her to complete the transaction. Already feeling restored, I followed the hand-drawn map through the campground. Beneath four towering trees I found my home for the night.

With the last dregs of my energy I put up my tent and made my home for the night. Out of the corner of my eye I noticed the towering figure of a man standing by a

large white van. He was watching me as I fussed with the
ground sheet, bending over in nothing but my lycra shorts
and neon-yellow sports bra. I tried to ignore him but felt
compelled to look up and nod in polite acknowledgement
that we would be neighbours for the night.

His arms were crossed over his broad chest, his head
shaved down to the skin, and above his lip was a thick
handlebar moustache that dropped to beneath his jawline.
He wore small, round glasses that magnified his beady
eyes. He continued to stare, and I continued to ignore him.
Then, through his whiskers, he said, 'You look like you
could use a whisky.'

At this I stood tall, placed my hands on my hips and
said, 'You know, I think you could be right.'

He sniggered, his moustache quivering, and in a gruff
drawl he continued, 'Well, you're welcome to join me and
my son for dinner tonight. We've got plenty of beer, whisky,
pork chops, potatoes, anything you like.'

At the mention of his son I dropped my guard.

'Yeah, Chase – he's running around with the other kids
right now. He's only five. We're on a father-son camping
weekend – some bonding time away from his mom, ya
know.'

The sense of pride in his voice turned poisonous at the
mention of the absent mother. I didn't ask, but instead said,
'Thank you, that would be really nice. It's been quite a
long day.'

'My name's Red, by the way, as in Redwood. My real
name's Dave, but my friends call me Red.' He held out his
hand and shook mine, clicking the joints in my palm with
his grip.

'Nice to meet you, Red,' I said. 'My name's Jo.'

'Jo? Hmm, Miss Jo. Nice you to meet you.'

At that moment Chase careened across the dirt and stopped, panting, at Red's feet.

'Chase,' his father said, 'meet our new friend, Miss Jo.'

I finished pitching my tent and headed for the campground pool. The water was cloudy with chlorine, sunscreen, and whatever debris the three dozen kids had deposited in the water, but I didn't care. A pair of teenagers were canoodling in the deep end, while their younger friends teased and splashed at them to stop. I submerged myself under the lukewarm water and listened as my breath formed loud bubbles around my ears, blocking out the sound of the screaming and laughter. Next I took a shower and washed my clothes, scrubbing the encrusted salt from my shorts, shirt and bra with the same bar of soap I used to wash my skin, stomping them on the shower floor with my feet to rinse.

Once dressed in my long leggings and merino-wool jersey, I headed for the Old English Pub, one of the main attractions of the campsite. It was uncannily familiar, reminiscent of the pubs I knew growing up in London. The same smell of stale cigarettes, beer-soaked carpet, wood varnish and lime cordial permeated the small, kitsch bar. The seats were royal blue, the floor covered in worn-out paisley carpet; there was a framed photograph of the Queen, and behind the bar bottles of Malibu, Baileys, Midori and vodka were displayed like works of art. I sat on a broken stool and waited for the bartender to appear.

Through the kitchen door walked an elderly lady, her purple hair tightly permed. She wore a neat blouse underneath a dark-blue cardigan. 'What can I get you, love?' She asked in a thick cockney accent.

'Wait, you're English?' I replied.

'Course I am. I own this place. This is a traditional British pub.'

That much was obvious, but I was happy for her elaboration.

'Me too,' I told her. 'I'm from London – Crystal Palace.'

'Really? You don't sound like a South Londoner,' she challenged. 'I'm from Hackney. *East* London.'

'I used to live there too, years ago,' I replied, happy to find common ground.

She pulled me a pint of lager and slid it across the bar, spilling the foamy head onto the frayed paper bar mat.

'It's on the house, love. It's my birthday today,' she smiled, her eyes disappearing for a moment in a field of wrinkles.

'Really? That's wonderful. Happy birthday!' I toasted.

'Thanks. That's right, I'm eighty-two years old today. Almost as old as the Queen!' She stood tall with the grace and elegance of a woman in her thirties, the twinkle in her blue eyes as bright as the Milky Way. She pulled herself a beer and we drank together, chatting like old friends.

It was almost ten o'clock. I hadn't seen Red or Chase since I was in the pool, so decided I would probably be dining alone tonight after all. I'd bought a can of beans from the little shop at the reception, and sat at my picnic table with my head torch on, happily eating them with a spork.

Then, out of the darkness, Chase appeared. 'Miss Jo, Miss Jo, have you got the whisky?' His voice was high-pitched, his breath rapid.

'Um, no,' I replied. 'I think your dad must have it.'

He blinked his dark brown eyes at me, then turned and disappeared into the blackness again. I could hear his feet scuttling to where Red was bent over the fire pit. Their figures cut ghoulish silhouettes in the orange glow.

I took the fire as an invitation and stepped over to their abode. On the table was an impressive display of beer, whisky and Gatorade. Also a pile of raw potatoes, which lolled about the table like abandoned golf balls, a pile of slimy, uncooked pork chops, a bag of marshmallows, packets of chocolate and tubes of Sour Patch Kids. I was glad I had taken the initiative and eaten that can of beans.

'Take a seat, Miss Jo, make yourself at home,' Red drawled, flamboyantly motioning towards the bench as though it were dressed in the finest linen. He handed me a glass, picked up the bottle of Jack Daniels and passed it to Chase. 'Go on, Chase, pour Miss Jo a drink,' he ordered jovially.

I held I out my glass and giggled at the sight of Chase trying to tip the heavy bottle, his small hands gripping tightly to the black label. He poured generously, almost losing his grip, and I had to tip the bottle back upright to stop the flow.

Red laughed. 'That's my boy!'

'Cheers!' I raised my glass to Red's, then we each clinked our glass against the bottle, which Chase was still holding.

Red drank. I drank. Then Chase, tipping back the bottle, which was bigger than his head, drank. Tears streamed down his small face, and he started to cough and splutter. Almost reflexively he reached for the marshmallows and stuffed a handful in his mouth, perhaps to douse the fire of the whisky burning his young throat.

Red laughed hard, his cackle resounding off the night sky, and Chase, encouraged by his father, took another swig, this time two large gulps. The boy's tears reflected the red of the fire.

'Okay, okay, that's enough,' said Red finally, reaching over for the bottle and removing it from Chase's grip.

I sat there frozen, unsure of what to do – unsure of what I was witnessing.

Chase's face was a mask of dancing shadows and light, his childish cheeks pearlescent and pale. He looked up at me quizzically, his eyes still watering, and said, 'How old are you, Miss Jo?'

'How old do you think I am?' I asked back.

'Seventeen?' he replied, his voice the essence of innocence.

'Ha, no, not quite. But thanks,' I chuckled. 'How old are you, Chase?'

He furrowed his brow, scrunching up his nose and mouth, and held up his fingers in front of his face. 'One, three, four, six, two. Um...' His words were slurred and slow.

'Don't mind him,' Red interrupted, 'he's been drinking!' And with a frightful cackle the man threw back his head and fell off the bench. His jeans caught on the splinters, and he landed with his bare arse on the ground. He didn't bother to get up, but lay back and continued to laugh, his jeans around his knees.

I looked back at Chase, who was still trying to count to five on his hands, and I realised I had walked into a tragedy. 'I think it's time for bed,' I said sheepishly, trying to find a polite way out. The rest of the campsite was quiet. I thanked Red and Chase for their hospitality and excused myself, walking backwards towards my camp, not wanting to turn my back on the scene, though I felt powerless to do anything.

I unzipped my tent and climbed fully clothed into the relative safety of its cocoon. Shaken by my dubious neighbours, I surrounded myself with my belongings, tucking my bags around me to create some kind of protective forcefield. All seemed quiet outside, and I started to relax.

Just as I was settling in for sleep, a spotlight danced against the skin of my tent and I heard heavy footsteps above my head. Then thick and clumsy whispers, one high, one low, chanting, 'Miss Jo, Miss Jo – wake up, Miss Jo.'

It was Red and Chase. They were circling my tent, taunting me with whispers and torchlight. I froze in my sleeping bag, clutching my penknife with one hand and my racing heart with the other. I listened to their cloddish antics for a while and finally decided that the best thing I could do was block them out and try to sleep. I put on my noise-cancelling headphones, turned on a recording of my mum playing the Telemann concerto, and hoped they would leave me alone.

Soon, but not soon enough, sleep descended and brought this day to a close.

12

DONUTS AND TOUR DE CALIFORNIA

LEGGETT – MENDOCINO: 86 KILOMETRES

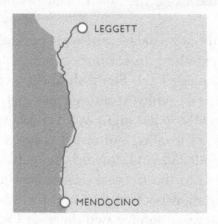

My alarm beeped loudly under my makeshift pillow. It was 6 a.m. I turned it off immediately, not wanting to wake my wretched neighbours. I was surprised to see the light of day again and wondered if everything had just been a dream. My bladder was full to bursting and pressed against my stomach uncomfortably. I'd not dared to relieve myself in the night.

I unzipped my tent slowly, trying not to make a sound. Tiptoeing barefoot to the bathrooms, I released my bladder, brushed my teeth and got dressed. I packed my tent and bags as quickly and quietly as I could. I could hear thunderous snoring coming from Red and Chase's tent, and not another soul seemed to be stirring in the campsite. I rolled my bike through the campground towards the exit and was gone by 6.30.

The road looked new, fresh with morning light and energy. I had only slept a few hours but I too felt new, and surprisingly strong after the intensity of the previous day. I flowed onto the quiet and empty road and said good morning to the trees, the smell of dawn filling me with optimism.

I'd left without breakfast, but was confident I would be able to get something to eat in Leggett, which wasn't far away now. I passed the Standish-Hickey campsite after a half-hour climb, which reassured me that I'd made the right decision to stop last night when I had. After Standish-Hickey the road levelled out and I enjoyed an easy sail, aided by a gentle tailwind, towards Leggett.

As I chatted to the trees, it dawned on me that I had no accommodation booked that night in Mendocino. I'd had no phone reception for two days, so I needed to find some wi-fi, log into my Warm Showers account and look for a vacancy, which might prove impossible at such short notice. I was also eager to contact my family to let them know I was alive and well.

A little before 8 a.m. I arrived in Leggett, which seemed to consist of only a gas station and a general store. I got off my bike carefully, hunger striking hard, and leaned it against the wall. The doors were still locked but the shutters were up, so I waited, peering in with my nose pressed against the glass door. From the back of the store a middle-aged woman sporting an 1960s bouffant appeared and waved welcomingly as she walked towards me. She unlocked the door and let me in.

'Good morning, come on in,' she sang, her fuchsia lipstick smeared across her front teeth.

I browsed the store for food supplies and bought some extra sunblock. Slowly locals began filling up the aisles, and the shopkeeper sang her welcome to each and every one of them.

'Excuse me,' I asked at the checkout counter, 'do you have wi-fi here?'

'Oh, no, sorry, darlin', we don't,' she apologised.

'Would you happen to have a phone that works? See, I'm biking alone down the West Coast right now, and I haven't been able to contact my family for some time as my phone doesn't work,' I explained hopefully.

Her painted eyebrows lifted. 'Oh, you poor love! Let's see,' she placed her hands on her hips, 'we do have a computer in the back. Maybe that would work for you? You gotta tell your ma and pa you're alright.'

'That would be fantastic. I'll just log onto my email and write my family a note to let them know I'm okay. Thank you!'

She walked me through the store, past the restrooms and into a large office, where another woman was sitting behind a desk.

'Sue, this is...I'm sorry, what was your name?'

'Jo,' I said.

'Jo? Oh, what a pretty name. Sue, this is Jo. She needs to log into her email and write her family a note.' Her hand was patting my shoulder as she spoke.

Sue smiled and, with arthritic hands, turned the computer around to me. 'I hope you know how to use this better than I do.'

I sat down and straightaway noticed a post-it note stuck next to the keyboard with a wi-fi network and password written on it. Neither Sue nor the other lady knew it was there. I logged onto the wi-fi on my phone and looked for shelter for the night, zooming in on the pins around Mendocino. There were only two to choose from, so I clicked on the pin nearest the ocean. The name that appeared was Jeremy Stone. I scrolled through his profile, which detailed his address, phone number and so on. It also noted that he'd like 'as much warning as possible'. I hoped ten hours would suffice. The tiny profile picture showed little detail, just a guy with a bike, and next to it the words 'Hope you have a safe journey and the adventure of your life'. Given my lack of options, I decided he was safe.

I sent him a message. 'Hi Jeremy, my name's Jo. I know this is rather short notice, but I am biking from Leggett to Mendocino today and wondered if you might be able to host me tonight? I have a tent and can camp in the backyard, no problem. My reception is spotty, so I hope we can connect at some point today. Cheers, Jo.'

Then I sent a message to my family to assure them I was alive. Sue seemed to have dozed off in her chair, the desk fan gently blowing her grey hair. I quietly thanked her and returned to the shop floor, which was now a hub of activity and smelled of freshly brewed coffee. My bike was as I'd left it, leaning against the wall outside, with a bunch of bananas balanced on the ukulele case.

Just as I was about to get on my bike, an older man with wild, white whiskers, carrying a bag of donuts in the crook of his arm like a swaddled baby, approached. 'Portland to LA, huh?' he said, pointing at my inscribed ukulele case. 'Where ya headed today?'

Reluctant to tell this complete stranger where I was going, I just said, 'I'm headed south.'

He kept pushing. 'Oh yeah? To Fort Bragg? Or further?'

'I'm planning to get to Mendocino, actually,' I admitted, deciding that maybe I could ask his advice. 'I take that road there, right?' I pointed to the left, beyond the gas station.

'You sure do, but you got some big hills to climb between

here and Fort Bragg, you know?' He lifted his head and looked down his reddened nose at me. 'You better be careful, it's a steep and narrow climb for the next twenty-seven miles. Cars can barely get over those hills!' His tone was a cloying combination of support, concern and condescension.

'Really? Well, I'll be just fine. I've already made it all the way from Portland. Besides, I actually enjoy climbing hills,' I said curtly, wanting to get on my way.

He smiled, his whiskers rising towards the crow's feet at the edge of his light-grey eyes. 'Good on you, girl.'

I pointed at the bag he was clutching, changing the subject. 'What kind of donuts do you have there?'

'Oh, just some old-fashioned mini donuts. I woke up this morning and realised that I hadn't had a donut in twenty-five years. So, for no good reason at all, I decided today would be the day I break the donut fast. They're not bad, actually – would you like one?'

I was starving. 'Yes, please. I haven't a donut since I was a kid. My brothers and I used to challenge each other to eat jam donuts without licking our lips.'

He opened the grease-stained paper bag and handed it to me, and we stood there chewing contentedly on the sweet, doughy goodness.

'You know, you remind me of my daughter,' he said out of the blue. 'My name's Mac, by the way.' He pointed again at my ukulele case. 'I'm also a musician – amateur, but I love music.'

'Nice to meet you, Mac; my name's Jo. Thanks for the donuts. They'll get me over the hill no problem. I better get on my way now, before the sun gets too hot.'

'Okay, Jo. Good luck. I'll wave you on over the hill.'

With that I saddled up and wheeled out of the general store's parking lot, and turned left towards Fort Bragg.

The road between Leggett and Fort Bragg was an endless helter-skelter climb towards heaven. It started to creep up almost immediately, the incline a steady 25 degrees. I clicked down to granny gear and remained there for the next three hours. Just as I got into a groove, the road would turn back on itself in a sharp switchback. Sun on my face, sun on my back, sun on my face, sun on my back.

Cars crawled along beside me, giving me a wide berth. Some cheered me on with shouts through the window or light honks. For the first time, the drivers seemed to exude empathy for what I was going through. I heard a horn's *peep-peep* and looked around to see Mac waving encouragement through the open window of his bright-red Prius. I waved back and smiled, calling back, 'Thanks again for the donuts!'

I could hear cars' engines struggling against the gradient, but my bike seemed to be made for the hill. I felt strong, energised by an oceanic release of endorphins and adrenaline. With my bodyweight over my handlebars, I heaved my bike to and fro like I was trying to capsize a raft, never stopping the upward momentum. The trees created a dappling of shade, their bark and leaves expelling sweetness which I gulped in through my mouth and nose. The road today was a stark contrast to yesterday's dusty and aggressive highway.

Cranking away in granny gear, I didn't dare stop pedalling for fear that I wouldn't be able to start again. Every so often I would look down at the map to see where the blue dot that was me was in relation to the ocean. There was still a lot of land between me and it. After an hour of strenuous cycling, the road plateaued and the trees opened to reveal a breathtaking panorama to the west, and a blanket of cloud below.

A couple had parked their car on a small pullout and were taking photos.

'Is this the top?' I asked as I rolled towards them.

'Not quite – still a little ways to go,' the lady replied, lightheartedly.

I waved at them in thanks as I passed, and a little later the road tipped downward again. Now I had to be over the top, and I started to pedal fast, letting the wind cool me. I plummeted down the hill, carefully navigating around each sharp bend until the road led me beneath the fog. The taste of the air changed from sweet and dry to salty, cool, alive. I salivated as I hastened towards the ocean.

For a while I had the road to myself once more. Then behind me I heard the *putt-putt* of a motorbike. Dressed in head-to-toe leathers, a motorcyclist slowed as he approached, his face concealed behind his black visor. He didn't zoom past as I thought he would; rather, he rode alongside me, his anonymous face turned towards me. I kept my head forward, fiercely disregarding his presence.

When he didn't move on, I pointed ahead without looking at him, as if to say, 'Go on, go!' He revved his engine twice and drove on. I was mildly relieved until, 500 metres ahead, I noticed his bike parked on the side of the road, leaning on its kickstand. I stopped in my tracks. There was no other traffic. I was alone. 'Fuck,' I hissed at the fog.

I squinted to see if I could spot where the rider was. Just then he stepped out from the bush, zipping up his fly. I waited until he was back on his bike before riding on, and watched as he disappeared ahead. I felt sure this was the end of the story, but moments later he returned, riding towards me on the other side of the road, then he made a U-turn and drove behind me again.

I was livid, my fury overriding my fear. I stopped my bike and turned to face him. As he grew close, I screamed at the top of my lungs, '*Go a-way!*' fiercely hitting each syllable.

He took one last look at me through his blackened visor, revved his throttle and sped off. The fog prickled on the back of my neck. I biked on, cautiously preparing for another confrontation, but thankfully I didn't see him again.

The road continued, and still there was no sign of the ocean. I checked the map and saw that there remained a vast chunk of land between me and it. Insidiously, the road began to climb again, and soon I was back to pushing and pulling my bike up endless switchbacks, reaching the cloudless sky above the trees again an hour later. The road was testing me, and I looked around for tricksters hiding in the trees. Were the donut man, the motorcyclist, the smiling couple, even the fog, all characters placed here to create this surrealist composition? My perception was warping with the haze of the morning, and I wondered if I would ever see the Pacific again.

I considered all this as I stood on the second plateau of the morning, high above the fog and the tree line. I took a moment and had a snack. It was now nearing 11 a.m. I had climbed almost 40 kilometres since Leggett, just as Mac had promised I would. I pedalled on for the final push.

As the ground started to tip downward, I surrendered to the gravitational pull towards the fog. The corners were deathly sharp, and every few metres I pumped the brakes to control my speed. The pain in my knee was starting to bother me again so I sat in my saddle, lifting the weight off my feet. My front wheel shivered as I reached speeds of over 50 kilometres per hour. The fog wrapped its cool blanket around me, and the dark forest curled inwards like hands around a fortune teller's orb. It was claustrophobic, disorientating and exhilarating.

Up ahead, the sky brightened, the trees opened and there, like a mirage, was the horizon. I stared into the space ahead of me, not daring to believe what I saw was true. And then the sky opened up completely and I came to a stop above a cliff that dropped down to the vast, endless, Pacific Ocean. I felt like Snow White escaping the enchanted forest.

'Woo hoo,' I yelped. 'Hello, ocean, it's me! I'm back! It's so nice to see you here.' The sound of my voice seemed like a childish version of my own. I propped my bike against the guard rail that separated the road from the hundred-foot drop down to the dancing waves below, and cried with relief. It seemed that, no matter how dehydrated I might be, I always had a reservoir of tears.

The bars of signal on my phone had returned, so I checked Warm Showers to see if I had a place to stay. There was a message in my inbox.

'Hi Jo, sure, no problem. You can stay here tonight. Just give me a call when you know your ETA.'

I dialled the number before my phone could lose its signal again. It rang a few times before a voice on the other end of line answered: 'This is Jeremy.'

'Hi, Jeremy, it's Jo. The Warm Showers girl.'

'Oh, hi, great to hear from you. Where are you now?' His voice was friendly.

'I'm standing above the ocean right now, on the corner where the road meets the water again. I just made it over the hill from Leggett,' I said, unsure of exactly where I was.

'No way! You realise that you just successfully conquered the tour de California? That makes you a superhero, ya know?' he said, and I could hear him smiling. I was heartened by the notion that I had reached superhero status, and smiled back.

'I hope to make it to Mendocino by four p.m. It's another sixty kilometres, so it shouldn't take me too long.'

'Perfect. See you then. Happy trails,' he said, and hung up.

I put my phone down and turned to see a large white van approaching. Red wore dark glasses and was focused on the road ahead, gripping the steering wheel with both hands. He didn't notice me standing there, even with my bright-yellow bags and neon-yellow jacket.

At first I couldn't see Chase, then he appeared at the front passenger window and looked straight at me. In the moment we locked eyes I saw a question in his face, a glimmer of recognition clouded with confusion, as though he'd seen me only in a dream. I didn't wave. I followed them with my eyes, and watched as they vanished into the horizon.

With the Pacific Ocean to my right, I no longer felt lost; I knew I was travelling in the right direction. I pedalled onward to Mendocino, tired but positive. The coastline rolled along, steep and unforgiving. Many small trees lined the road. In every twist of bark and green leaf I saw something new. It was as though I had a magnifying glass up to my eyeball and I could pick out every detail on every tree that I passed. I blinked and looked again, riding slowly, staring in disbelief. I was witnessing the beauty of these trees as if for the first time. Could it be that my eyesight had sharpened on this journey from looking outward every day, travelling at a speed between walking and driving? Could it be that my brain had started to adjust my visual cortex to the speed of a bicycle?

I marvelled at this concept, and for a few minutes forgot my fatigue. My knee, however, was angry, and duly reminded me of this with every pedal rotation. I was now only 25 kilometres shy of Mendocino, and I felt like I was pedalling backwards. I looked miserably at my speedometer: I was crawling along at 8 kilometres per hour, running on empty and wincing in pain. I came to an inelegant halt, my bike slumping to the side, and I let it crash to the ground as I hopped off. I looked back up the road to study the passing vehicles. In that moment I decided that if I saw a camper van or truck go by, I would hail it down and ask for a ride. I had reached my body's limit.

A vintage camper trundled towards me, and I stuck my thumb out and smiled. To my surprise, its indicator blinked orange and the van stopped. The side door slid open and I saw a gleaming smile. 'Need a ride, do you? Where are you trying to get to?' a lady in a blue cashmere sweater asked.

'Yes, please. To Mendocino, if possible?'

'Sure thing, come on in. We must apologise for the smell – we've been making bacon sandwiches,' she said, still grinning.

'No worries at all – it actually smells great. Thanks so much for stopping.'

In the driver's seat was a handsome, spindly gentleman, his salt-and-pepper hair cut short, and his tanned skin indicating a life lived on the Californian coast.

'We're just heading home from a weekend road trip,' he told me by way of greeting. 'We're celebrating our thirty-fifth wedding anniversary.'

The couple looked barely over forty. Both husband and wife were lean and spritely, and clearly living the life of two young lovers. They drove me and my bike 15 kilometres down the coast, chatting all the way. They were high on their love for life and one another. I asked them to drop me a few kilometres shy of Mendocino so I could at least arrive there on my bike. We chose a random spot on the side of the road, where I disembarked from their love boat and waved as they drove away.

I pedalled the last stretch into Mendocino, mindful of my exhaustion, but all the while absorbing the beauty of the coastline. I free-wheeled down the main street, passing tempting cafes and gift stores, and turned left. I arrived at what I thought was Jeremy's address, but it seemed to be a museum. I called his phone to confirm.

'I think I'm here, but I'm not really sure,' I said warily.

'Great, you made it. I was getting ready to send out a search party,' he chuckled.

'Do you live in a museum?' I asked.

'I live in the water tower just behind the museum. Wheel your bike up the driveway, and I'll be right down.'

I looked up, and towering above the museum's tiled roof was a fairytale picture of an old wooden water tower.

13

WATER TOWER

MENDOCINO – BODEGA BAY – MILL VALLEY:
250 KILOMETRES (KILOMETRES ACTUALLY RIDDEN: 74)

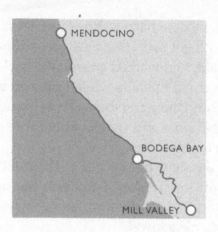

I pushed my bike up the driveway, which was overgrown
with weeds. Looking up, I saw a kind face smiling down
from a doorway high on the tower. Jeremy stood with
his hands on the banisters, and for a moment neither of
us moved. I waved, breaking the stillness, and he walked
down the wooden steps that clung to the edge of the tower.
We greeted with a handshake and he looked at my bike.

'You're travelling light, I see?' he joked. 'Well, look, you
can set up your tent in the yard, or I can just pull up this
pop-up tent and you won't have to set yours up at all.
Might be easier for you that way.'

At this he pulled on a handle and released a solid-topped
pop-up shelter fit for car camping. As soon as it opened, a
spray of maggots fell out; in every crevice was a city of the

wriggling yellow worms. We both jumped back in disgust, then laughed.

'Shit, I guess I haven't used this tent for a while,' Jeremy apologised.

'I'll just set my own tent up over here, if that's okay?' I deferred.

'Would you like to have a shower first, or…?' he asked.

'It's okay. I'll get everything set up and then I can relax properly,' I said, and walked around the back of the tower.

Jeremy returned upstairs while I pitched my tent in the long grass behind the water tower. I was proud of myself for making a cosy home and was looking forward to sleeping in it in peace tonight.

I climbed the steps one by one to the front door, relying on the banister for support; I couldn't put any weight on my knee. I knocked lightly and Jeremy whisked the door open, handing me a towel.

'Come on in,' he said. 'The bathroom is right there. The water should be hot.' He spoke and moved quickly, with a certain nervousness. He welcomed me into a humbly decorated octagonal room, the only pieces of furniture being a small wooden table with two chairs, and a red-velvet couch shaped like a pair of lips. 'I'm going to go see what my sons are up to downstairs. Hopefully they haven't turned the place upside-down. Help yourself to the shower and shampoos. Make yourself at home.'

I stood holding the soft towel, listening to his footsteps reverberating through the walls as he skipped down the steps outside. I hadn't noticed his sons when I'd arrived, but now I could hear their high voices through the floorboards.

I spent a long time in the dark-blue-tiled shower, beneath the stream of the clear, warm water. My skin was caked with sweat and sunscreen, and as the water broke it down

I could taste the salt of my sweat in my mouth, mingling with the soap from my hair. I got dressed in leggings and a tank top, and put on a light layer of makeup and a pair of earrings. I felt the need to be attractive and transform myself from exhausted cyclist to elegant woman again.

I stood in front of the bathroom mirror as the steam on its surface dissipated. My arms were more muscular than I was used to, and my face slightly swollen from dehydration and exposure to the wind and sun. The mascara and earrings looked out of place on me now, so I removed them, feeling foolish for wanting to make an effort. Then, after splashing cold water on my face, I reapplied the mascara and put my earrings back on. I went out into the living room and sat on the edge of the red-lips couch.

Jeremy was standing by the kitchen counter with his back to me. The muscles in his shoulders were defined through his T-shirt, the veins in his forearms prominent as he sliced cheese and fruit, and placed them creatively onto a wooden board.

'Would you like a glass of wine?' he asked, turning and handing me the snacks. 'Here, I made these for you.'

His face was narrow, his cheekbones high. We sat together at the table by the window, and I noticed something in his eyes that I recognised. The circumference of his mossy-green iris was a deep blue, and enclosing his pupils was a ring of bright yellow – just like my own eyes.

'What?' he asked, noticing me staring at him.

'Oh, nothing,' I said, snapping out of my trance. 'Thanks so much for this. I feel much better already.'

Before the sun disappeared for the day, I walked down to the edge of the cliffs bordering Mendocino and watched as the turquoise ocean water rippled around the rock formations that jutted out below. The fog was rolling back in, kissing the soft blue sky with its droplets, bringing with it a coolness that seeped through my layers of clothing. Just before I stood to leave, I was visited by a lone dolphin, which swam like a silver arrow beneath the surface, twirling in the evening light.

Later that evening, I told Jeremy about the dolphin.

'That means you must be blessed on this journey, because there hasn't been a dolphin sighting here all year,' he told me without a hint of irony. Then, with a dramatic pause: 'Jo, I think you've entered the Pure Zone.'

'The Pure Zone? What's that?' I asked, raising my eyebrows.

Jeremy sat back in his chair, placed his hands flat on the table and let out a sigh. 'The Pure Zone is where you are. It's the state of completeness, of being absolutely at one and present with your surroundings, being in tune with the universe with no expectation. Almost expressionless. Totally transparent. I think you've entered this sacred space, and pretty quickly, it seems.' His words were like an offering. 'You only hit the road a week ago, right?' he asked.

'Almost two weeks ago, actually. The third of August was my first day on the road,' I told him.

'Makes sense. You're going through a lot doing a trip like this, especially alone. It's no wonder you have reached Pure Zone status already. You obviously have a very open spirit. It's exciting, Jo. Sky's the limit from here on in.'

His tone was both mystical and completely ordinary, and I couldn't tell if this was an elaborate pick-up line or a genuine gift. Whichever it was, his words justified the inexplicable sensation of heightened awareness and clear-mindedness I had been experiencing, and I thanked him for his contribution.

I didn't have to sleep in my tent that night after all. Jeremy's sons went to their mother's house, so the large bedroom downstairs was vacant. I now had my own bathroom and a king-size bed all to myself, while my tent lay open and unused on the floor, drying out from the evening dew. I slept the sleep of the dead.

In the morning, I almost fell out of bed as I tried to stand up, my left knee giving way beneath me. Jeremy knew my knee was in a bad way, as I'd arrived with my leg bandaged from shin to thigh. He'd offered to drive me as far as Mill Valley, a small town just north of San Francisco, where he worked a construction job. I'd told him I would sleep on the offer. Accepting this ride would cut two full days, and more than 150 kilometres, from my journey. My record of accepting rides – now an average of almost one a day – was starting to resemble what I saw as failure. So I declined Jeremy's offer, assuring him that after such a good sleep I would make it to my destination of Gualala, 83 kilometres south of Mendocino. Deep down, I wasn't so sure.

He understood my determination and didn't try to convince me otherwise, even as I hobbled around. We hugged tightly on the driveway where we had shaken hands less than twenty-four hours earlier, and I waved him adieu.

I did feel a lot better for the good sleep and hearty dinner. My knee was strapped up tightly and I used my right leg for most of the turning power. The first few kilometres out of Mendocino were mellow, but soon the Pacific Coast Highway began twisting and elevating ferociously, whipping back and forth like an agitated snake, its corners sharp and steep. Just as I free-wheeled down one hill I had to pedal hard to maintain momentum up the next, using my arm strength and right leg to keep the pressure off my left. The fog was low and I was glad for the cool air.

I had grown so used to the discomfort in my knee, my pain threshold increasing every day, that it was only when I looked down to see it swollen out of proportion, the kneecap soft and mushy, that I gave in and accepted that I had done some significant damage.

I sent Jeremy a text: 'I think I need a ride after all. But please don't rush. I am going to bike as far as I can, so just find me whenever you drive by later this afternoon.' I was determined to experience this coastline on my bike. With the knowledge that I would be picked up soon, I pushed on, keeping half an eye on my ever swelling knee, and enjoying the ride through gritted teeth.

After cycling 45 kilometres I reached Point Arena Lighthouse and stopped for lunch. I sat on a grassy patch in front of the restaurant and ate my own basic supplies: a brown banana wrapped in a tortilla, and another wrap filled with cheese and capsicum. Satiated, I continued along the road. Fiery-red fields stretched as far as the eye could see towards the ocean, contrasting starkly with the marble-grey sky. I was feeling good and was about to send Jeremy another message cancelling my SOS when his silver Toyota Tacoma stopped in front of me.

'You're here already?' I exclaimed, half-disappointed.

'Knight in shining armour, at your service, m'lady,' he said in a faux British accent, and bowed. He looked up and, seeing my reticence, said, 'How about I take your luggage and you ride on as far as you like?'

'Really? But I'll be way slower than you.'

'It's okay, I'm not in a rush. Go on, enjoy yourself!' he insisted.

With that I stripped my bike of everything but a single water bottle and wobbled onward, my bike feeling like a feather in comparison to its usual elephantine self. After a while I was whizzing along the road, grinning from ear to ear, barely putting any effort into the wheels. I had a tailwind, no luggage and immense power in my body, thanks to all the kilometres I had ridden thus far. Without the extra weight to pull, my knee seemed to work more-or-less fine.

I continued for a further 15 kilometres until I reached Anchor Bay. I spied Jeremy's truck parked by a coffee shop and pulled over to join him. I was ready. I had proved myself enough for one day – and now that I had stopped, the searing pain from my knee was flooding through me again.

We drove in silence, Jeremy staring at the road, while I gazed longingly at the ocean.

'Hey, Jeremy, how do you feel about jumping in for a swim?' I suggested.

'Swim? But it's freezing in there!' he said, stating the obvious.

'I know, but it's the ocean. We can't *not* swim in it,' I cajoled. 'Besides, the cold might be good for my knee.'

'Okay…You're crazy, ya know?' he stated flatly.

'I know.'

We continued towards Gualala Bay. I stuck my head out of the window, analysing each and every grade of the road, internalising the landscape and trying to imagine how it would feel to ride. We didn't stop at Gualala, instead continuing beyond Bodega Bay until I spied a beach access.

As soon as we'd parked, my inclination was to run down

to the water, but I could barely step out of the car. Jeremy helped me as I limped down the wooden steps to the sand. There was a large driftwood structure that served perfectly as a private changing room for me.

'Are you sure about this, Jo?' Jeremy pleaded. 'This is crazy! I never swim in the ocean up here. I'm too skinny!'

'As sure as I could ever be,' I said. 'Come on, it'll be great.'

I took the lead and limped across the untouched sand to the shoreline. The ocean was black-blue, and looked colder than cold. The first touch of icy water on my toes sent a tingle through me that rippled to the top my head. I walked in steadily, until the water was over my knees. Even as the cold took my breath away, I felt instant relief.

Jeremy danced and yapped as if he was walking on hot coals, simultaneously trying to escape the water as he approached it. The only thing for it was to dive head-first and let the water whip our breath out of our lungs and feed it to the fishes. We screamed and laughed like banshees. We were crazy.

We arrived in Mill Valley late. Jeremy had assured me I would have my own room and privacy. His friend's mother owned the house and was sleeping, and we entered through the back door. He showed me his bed and told me I could have it – he would sleep on the couch. I was too tired to argue or even question my safety, so I simply thanked him, brushed my teeth and lay down in the darkness of his room. I listened as he rustled around next door, trying to make himself comfortable on the couch.

My phone lit up with a message: 'Sleep well.'

'Thanks, Jeremy, you too. Goodnight.'

My phone flashed again: 'I'd sleep better knowing you were near me.'

My heart skipped a beat, and my skin tingled with a strange combination of apprehension and arousal.

'If you want to sleep in here, it's okay. You can,' I replied.

'Only if you're sure,' he texted.

I lay there in the dark, the moon cutting a sliver of silver through the thin curtain, listening to the silence that would soon be broken.

For the next two days I dwelled in a twilight zone of hedonistic recovery, sleeping the daytime hours away in the sunshine by the pool, an icepack on my knee, and exploring San Francisco by car at night. I wasn't going to fight it.

On my last day in Mill Valley, I had been invited to visit the Kala Brand Music Company's ukulele HQ in Petaluma, a short drive to the north. They had arranged for me to record one of my songs live on video as part of their Kala Brand online series.

I drove Jeremy's truck to the industrial estate where the office was and was welcomed by Nick Hernandez, one of the Kala representatives. It was like going into the Disneyland of ukuleles, and I had the honour of playing my choice of one of their beautifully handcrafted instruments. At the end of my visit, Nick told me to choose any instrument I liked. I pointed at a cedar-topped baritone.

'That's a great instrument,' he said, taking it down off the shelf and handing it to me. 'Here, try it out.'

Its tone was warm, rounded, rich. I fell in love.

'It's all yours,' Nick continued. 'Our gift. We love how you play – your songs are awesome, and your Great Song Cycle tour is such a fantastic story, so we're happy to support you and your music.'

'Really?' I gasped. 'But that's amazing!'

'Here,' he said, handing me the long-necked soprano I had played in the video. 'You should have this one too. You made it sound great.'

He arranged for both instruments to be mailed to my home in Brooklyn, as I couldn't carry another thing on my bike. They would be waiting, like a promise of the success of this journey, on my return.

14

GOLDEN GATE

MILL VALLEY – MISSION DISTRICT, SAN FRANCISCO:
35 KILOMETRES

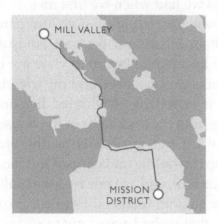

The 18th of August dawned and, according to my itinerary, I was due to be in San Francisco. I had been on the road for a full two weeks now, and had biked over 950 kilometres since leaving Portland. The swelling and pain in my knee had finally subsided and I was feeling fit and fully healthy for the first time on this ride.

The time I'd spent in Mill Valley had been a bubble of recovery and rest, but I knew that I could not stay – nor did I want to. I was ready to be reunited with my mission, to be back on the road in my solitude, and back on stage as well. I had a show in Oakland the next day, at the Octopus Literary Library, with a pianist I was yet to meet, and was chomping at the bit to play music again. Biking was only supposed to be half the adventure, though it seemed to be all-consuming.

I said goodbye to Jeremy early in the morning, just as the sun was settling in the sky. It was not a sad farewell, rather one of celebration at having met. We knew that we would see each other again, though we did not know when. We embraced, exchanged a single kiss on the cheek, and waved as we had when we first met.

My bike was packed, all five yellow panniers in their place, the chain oiled, and the seat adjusted to make it easier on my knee. I had begun to view my bike not as an *it* at all. My bike was my steed and my friend, ever patient, ever sturdy, ever reliable. I wheeled her down the steep steps leading from the back door of the house with a series of loud clunks. I put my hands on the brakes, stepped over and onto the saddle and clipped in. The morning was sweet and peaceful, and as I released the brakes my wheels slid along the smooth road and I smiled, luxuriating in the warm breeze that rushed across my face.

Everything was new again. I could hear the pages turning. I felt stronger than ever, my body now perfectly adapted for long-distance cycling. I had ridden so many kilometres in varying degrees of pain that, now the pain was absent, I barely remembered the struggle, fear and concern, and instead sailed along with an overwhelming sense of elation.

I followed the cycle path that wove through the suburbs of Mill Valley towards the Golden Gate Bridge. Ahead of me I noticed another cycle tourist, conspicuous with a loaded trailer and an American flag sticking out from the back of his seat. As I got closer, I noticed, written in thick black pen on a cardboard placard stuck to the back of his trailer, the words: 'Biking Around America For Cancer'.

He wore a pair of old jeans that were worn at the knees, lace-up sneakers and a baggy T-shirt. His helmet was askew and his face a map of everything he had lived through. He did not appear particularly fit, though he rode with the steady pace of the tortoise that would make it to the finish line.

As soon as I was next to him, he started talking to me. His name was Stephen. He had biked across the country more than ten times already, and had no plans to stop. His destination was the road, and as long as he was alive he would be cycling. As he rattled off stories of his new life as a full-time long-distance cyclist, I signed his book, which was filled with the signatures of the thousands of people he had met on his travels. He lived off donations from strangers, family and friends, and appeared to be a very happy man.

We rode slowly alongside one another for a few miles until our paths diverged. I wondered if I would see him again down the road, but I did not.

As I approached the Golden Gate Bridge, a few dozen day-tripping cyclists, clad in head-to-toe lycra, and riding carbon-fibre bikes that weighed less than my handlebar bag, whizzed past me; now I felt like the tortoise. Beyond them was a sight that defied belief. Looming high above the fog were the iconic struts of the red-iron bridge, its vast cables sweeping majestically across the bay. I was giddy at the sight of it, a postcard-perfect image in front of my own eyes. I knew, too, that the Golden Gate Bridge marked the halfway point between Portland and Los Angeles.

Only a few days ago I wasn't sure if I would make it here on my two thin wheels, but now I could hear the traffic of cars rumbling across the bridge from north to south. Every struggle, challenge and discomfort thus far felt worth it, and I was struck by how easy it really was to bike to San Francisco. My perception of space, time and effort was changing by the day, and the more hardships I overcame, the easier and more possible everything seemed to be.

I walked my bike onto the north side of the bridge, joining the throng of tourists taking pictures and pointing into the canvas of clouds. The fog was thick and hung low, like fat grapes on an old vine; you could almost reach out and touch it. Rolling my bike slowly, and weaving between pedestrians, I made my way into San Francisco.

15

ALL A BLUR

'Why is the last hill always the steepest?' I asked myself, craning my neck and then slumping my shoulders exaggeratedly as I looked up towards my San Franciscan home-away-from-home.

My friends Jane and Roy lived in a beautiful, historical house in Bernal Heights, on an inconsolably steep hill that stretched upward from the Mission District. The only thing stopping me from my destination was this final stretch of road, which tilted skyward at what felt like a 50-degree angle. My gears had been in granny mode for the last few miles through the steep streets of the Mission District, but as I went to push down on my pedals for this final hill, my front wheel started to lift off the ground.

Defeated, I climbed off my saddle and pushed my loaded bike. The metal cleats on my shoes slipped backwards on the tarmac as I pushed against gravity, my hands sweaty in my gloves. I laughed almost maniacally as I recalled the endless climbs of the previous days, enjoying the pithiness of this urban challenge.

It is difficult for me to recall the hours when I was not on my bike, the day-to-day details blurring into an impressionistic landscape, undefined, abstracted, yet still brilliant in colour, sheen and texture. San Francisco offered three further days of rest, recovery and reflection. I explored the city by foot, train and bus, moving through the world with the feeling that I had a secret I was giddy to share with whoever might listen. Stopping in a coffee shop patronised by millennials wearing oversized glasses, blue-tipped hair, transparent crop tops, denim dungarees and odd socks pulled high over their hand-detailed Converse, I ordered a cold brew. Before the super-strength coffee had reached the top of the plastic cup I had told the barista that I was a musician on tour down the West Coast on my bicycle. She gave me a look that seemed to imply simultaneously that she was impressed and didn't give a shit.

I walked out into the cool sunshine with my iced drink and ducked through the doors of a boutique clothing store to try on the silk mini-dress that hung in the window.

'This will be perfect for my next show!' I told the store owner. 'And it won't add any weight to my luggage,' I added, eager for her to invite me to tell her my secret too. I felt a need to talk about it – the reality of what I was going through was too big for me to bear alone. If I didn't tell anyone, it felt that it might disappear as if it were a dream. The more time I spent not biking, the quicker those kilometres seemed to fade in my mind like the afternoon fog.

Though I had started to develop the idiosyncratic look of a cyclist – uneven tan lines on my legs, wrists and a perpetually sunburnt nose – I couldn't simply point to my skin for proof, so I kept striking up conversations with complete strangers, bending their ears with tales of the redwood forests and the Pacific Coast Highway.

Word had started to reach the press that there was a young female musician riding down the West Coast to play concerts. In fact, many of the audience who came to my shows were there, they told me, because they 'had to see it with their own eyes'.

I walked into the Octopus Literary Library in Oakland on the 19th of August and there, waiting for me on the piano, was my FedEx box from Arcata. I was disproportionately excited to see it, and opened it like a child ripping into a

Christmas present. I had forgotten what I'd packed – clearly I hadn't needed any of it for my ride since Pepperwood – but I was still glad to see my loop pedal and little black dress again, though less so to see the dozen Clif Bars I had packed away.

Slowly the room filled with curious faces, people willing to take a chance on a new and unknown musical offering. The modest crowd listened intently, hanging on my every lyric and note, my pianist creating the perfect counterpart to my melodies. The following day I played a solo show at the Red Poppy Art House in the Mission District, and again the intimate room filled with people who had come to support my music and me. The joy and elation I found in performing was like diving into the ocean, yet the undercurrent for me was not one of freedom. I clung to music with an emotion that also had the power to tear me apart.

Since my conception, music has flowed through my blood. I developed in my mother's womb to the vibrations of her violin. On the 13th of November 1985, the Bechstein piano belonging to my grandfather Peter was delivered, my father played a concert in central London, and I was born in the living room of our family home.

My relationship to music is akin to my relationship to breathing, eating and loving. It is a necessity, and has been associated with every aspect of my existence. For me, music has been the source of great joy and pain. Music is what took my parents away every few weeks on tour. Music is also what filled the house when they were home. Music is what sent me to sleep, and what I woke to. Music saved my grandmother's life in Auschwitz.

Sometimes I wish my relationship to music were simpler, lighter – that I could take it or leave it. But as I sang my songs to strangers and friends in the quaint bookstore in downtown Oakland, or in the cushion-strewn living room of the Red Poppy Art House the following night, I was reminded that music is the language that can transcend everything.

The day before I was due to leave San Francisco, I was invited to go sailing with an old friend, Bruce, whom I had known since my childhood summers in Carmel. As Bruce, his wife and I skimmed over the glassy bay, Bruce told me about a music cafe he had once played at in San Luis Obispo.

'When I was in my early twenties,' he told me, 'before I played classical trombone, I would sing on the stage in the back room of this cafe. I think it was called Lenny's or Linn's – or something like that. It's probably not there anymore, but you could find out on Google. Maybe you should check it out?'

My days in San Francisco had been luxurious: sleeping twelve hours a night in a beautiful house, walking the hills of the city, eating and drinking like a king, making new friends and playing music. I was starting to feel like part of the furniture, but this comfortableness was beginning to unnerve me, manifesting as a sort of cabin fever. My chest pulled me towards the great unknown again and I longed to be on my bike, travelling with the ocean by my side once more.

It was time to move on. My next stop was Half Moon Bay, just 53 kilometres south. I couldn't thank my hosts in San Francisco enough – their hospitality had been familial

and beyond generous. After I reloaded my luggage with
the contents of my FedEx box, my bike was heavy again. As
I stood at the top of the hill, I held my brakes tight against
the pull of gravity. I edged and squeaked my way down the
roller-coaster drop, and as soon as the street levelled out I
let go and zoomed towards Pacifica.

My route seemed straightforward enough, and I listened
to Siri as she directed me down the one-way street. After a
few hundred metres, though, she instructed me to 'make a
U-turn'. Obediently I did so – a complicated manoeuvre on
a heavily loaded bike across two lanes of city traffic – and
continued in the opposite direction. A few hundred metres
later she said again, 'Make a U-turn.' I was confused, but
again I made my way across the lanes. 'Make a U-turn,'
she said again, and again. I tried ignoring Siri and took a
different turn, but she rerouted me back onto the main road
and repeated, 'Make a U-turn.'

The fog was heavy and my mood fell. I'd ridden
3 kilometres and got nowhere. On the verge of tears,
I stopped outside a laundromat and ate a protein bar. Then
it occurred to me that there was one friend in San Francisco
I hadn't yet connected with. Dean had moved here from
New York only a few weeks earlier, so I tried his number to
see if he was free for a coffee. He worked for a concert series
called Sofar Sounds ('songs from a room') and had moved
to San Fransisco to head the team there. It was taking me
so long to get out of the city that I figured I might as well
take a break.

'Hello – who's this?' he answered, out of breath.

'Hey, Dean, it's Jo. Jo Wallfisch.'

'Oh, hey! Jo – sorry, I thought you were someone else.
I'm going through a bit of a work crisis right now.
What's up?'

'I'm in San Francisco – about to leave, actually – and wondered if you might be free to grab a coffee, like, right now?'

'Man, I wish I could. But I have to sort this thing out as soon as possible.' He sounded frantic.

'What's going on?'

'Well, I'm producing a concert tomorrow night at Hyde Street Studios,' he explained, 'but one of the bands just called and cancelled. So I'm desperately trying to find a musician to fill their place.'

'I'll do it,' I said, not skipping a beat.

'Whoa, really? You're still gonna be here tomorrow?' Dean sounded hopeful. 'But I thought you just said you were leaving?'

'That's just a small detail,' I said, eager for the opportunity to perform.

It dawned on me that I had no idea how I would get to the show if I left today, but I was certain I didn't want to spend another day off my bike, waiting.

'Okay, this is amazing,' Dean replied. 'I'm so glad you called me just now! I just have to make a couple phone calls to confirm that this is all good with the team. I'll get back to you in a few minutes. Cool?'

'Sure thing. I'll wait for your call,' I said, and hung up. I was excited by the latest challenge I had created for myself: how to get to Half Moon Bay today and back in time for the show tomorrow. I was determined to stick to my plan of leaving San Francisco. Worst case scenario, I would just have to ride north again.

I stood with my bike outside the laundromat, munching through my snacks as I waited for Dean to call back. To pass the time I tried googling the cafe Bruce had mentioned in San Luis Obispo. My search directed me to Linnaea's

Cafe, an artisanal coffee shop that presented live music most days of the week. It had to be the place. I wrote them a quick email via the contact form on their website, asking if I could play a show when I passed through in a few days. I wasn't confident of hearing back since it was such short notice, but I was excited to try.

As soon as I pressed 'send', Dean called back to say, 'You're all booked!'

Next I called Jeremy. 'Hey, how would you feel about driving down to Half Moon Bay tonight? And then, er, driving me back to San Francisco in the morning? I just booked another gig.'

He didn't hesitate to accept. With this new harebrained plan in place, I finally made it out of San Francisco.

My exit from the city was marked by the sight of a humpback whale breaching near the shore. I spied her tail between two apartment buildings as I came around a corner on the border of Pacifica, and then, with pure celebration, she flew out of the ocean and landed with an almighty splash. I was just as happy to be back on the road again.

16

FAR AWAY FROM ANY PLACE CALLED HOME

SAN FRANCISCO – HALF MOON BAY: 45 KILOMETRES

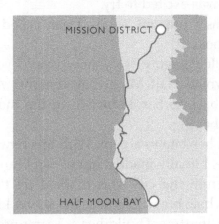

It was a black-and-white day, the sky a child's chalk drawing of clouds, the ocean a rippling of onyx, the road ahead a dragon's tongue stretching out towards the unknown. And then there was me: a neon-yellow beacon against the flat horizon, speeding along at 35 kilometres per hour with the gift of a tailwind. Not one car had passed me since Pacifica. My only company was the blowhole spray from a lone humpback whale swimming just offshore.

In the far distance I saw a figure walking along the hard shoulder, a silhouette against the grey curtain. I kept my focus on the shape of this stranger, unsure if I was seeing a mirage. As I drew closer, I was able to drink in the details of this man. He wore black jeans, a black denim jacket, black plimsoll shoes. His black hair was pulled back into a ponytail at the base of his neck, and a pair of black sunglasses carved two caves out of his chalk-white skin. He wore no bag upon his back, no expression upon his face. His only possession, aside from his clothes, appeared to be a small music player tucked into his breast pocket, with white headphones tucked into his ears. He did not look up as we momentarily shared the road, and after passing I soon forgot all about him.

I reached Half Moon Bay in the early afternoon, and pushed my bike to the hiker-biker area, once again pleased and surprised at having made it to my destination not only unscathed, but under my own steam. There were no other campers there yet, and I had pick of the sites. I placed my tent nearest the beach, and positioned it so the door opened to a view of the ocean. There were no showers at the campsite so I clambered into my bathing suit and ran down the dunes, across the cold white sand, and I didn't stop running until I was skipping over the freezing waves. I swam until I was numb to the core, until my skin was red and my lips were purple.

Before the shivers set in, I retreated from the water, not turning my back on the waves until my feet were firmly on dry sand again. As I turned around, my eyes still blurry from the salt, I saw, walking slowly along the pristine sand, untouched but for my scattered line of footprints, the same man.

I stood there trying to control my chattering teeth, and watched as he appeared to glide across the beach. As he crossed my path, seemingly unaware of my presence, I calculated that I had seen him more than 30 kilometres north of where we now stood. I followed him with my eyes, his footprints now presenting questions: *How did he get here? And where is he going?*

Jeremy arrived with a carload of food and we spent the

evening curled up against the cold and sleeping to the sound of the crashing waves. I was happy to see him again, but reticent to encourage the friendship any further, aware of the duplexity of my invitation. I woke at dawn, and before Jeremy opened his eyes I was already running back down towards the ocean, calling out, 'Dolphins! Dolphins!' Dozens of them were leaping joyously amid the translucent waves. Without hesitation I dived into the ocean and joined their morning congregation.

After breakfast, I piled my bags and bicycle into Jeremy's truck and, as though I was rewinding the tape, we drove north to San Francisco. I spent the car journey scribbling song lyrics into my journal.

'I think I've almost finished a new song,' I told him, excited to be creating again.

'Sweet. How does it go? Can you sing to me?'

'I think I might try to sing it tonight at the show,' I said, committing myself.

'Why don't you practise it now?' he suggested.

I reached in the back seat for my ukulele and took it from its case. Sitting cross-legged in the front passenger seat, my voice muffled against the wind that was rushing through the open windows, I sang my new song.

I'm going on a road trip,
winding down a well-worn path,
I change my background story
every time somebody asks.
I have worn so many masks.
Winding down the windows,
Letting in the breeze,
Breathing in the ashes of the burning redwood trees,
Time moves parallel with motion,
it's the traveller's disease,
We are all escapees.
There was the lady in the wheelchair,
Her mirage turned all too real,
As she rolled along the highway,
waiting for a car her life to steal.
I can't imagine how she feels.
And the father in the campsite
gives his child whisky rye,
Tip that bottle, son, that's right,
Til you see the starry sky.
What a fateful lullaby.
So now I see the world through different eyes,
As time slows down.
Forgetful dreams, make no more compromise,
This road knows no bounds.
I'm going on a road trip,
winding down a well-worn path,
I change my background story
every time somebody asks,
I have worn so many masks.

After breaking free of the centrifugal force of San Francisco, less than twenty-four hours later I was back. Jeremy dropped me, my bike and all my gear off at Dean's apartment building, then went on his way back to Mill Valley to work. I knocked on the front door and waited, my nose pressed to the warped glass window running down the side of the door frame. Soon I saw the marbled shape of Dean running down the stairs, and he opened the door.

'Hey! Wow, it's so good to see you!' he almost bellowed. 'Glad you could make it back. How'd ya get here? Come in, come in. Leave your bike here. Sorry, I'm in the middle of a million things. Coffee?'

I left my bike in the entranceway downstairs and took my five bags and ukulele upstairs. Dean lived with a work colleague in a large apartment. They'd just moved in and he had yet to get any furniture, aside from his bed and desk. I took one of the empty spare rooms and set up camp on the floor, laying out my mat and sleeping bag.

'Here's a pillow. Sorry I can't give you more than that,' Dean apologised, and threw a pillow across the hall from his room to mine. 'The other band who are playing tonight should be arriving any minute. They can sleep in the living room.'

Right on cue, the doorbell rang and Dean went downstairs.

'Whoa, dude, who's bike is that? It's so rad!' A man's voice dripping in California drifted up the stairs. 'Look, Erisy, someone biked here. Dude!' the voice concluded with emphasis.

Then a husky woman's voice floated up from the doorway, 'Oh, wow, yeah. Nice bike. Whose is it?'

'It's belongs to Jo,' Dean told them. 'She's just upstairs. You'll be sharing the bill with her tonight. She's on a tour of the West Coast right now, by bike.'

'Right on. Dude, that's awesome,' the lilting male voice replied.

The voices belonged to Raff and Erisy, two musicians from Santa Barbara. Suddenly feeling shy, I waited at the top of the stairs as they came up, but they greeted me with hugs as though we were old friends.

Raff was tall and beanpole thin, his long, wiry black hair knotted in a bun on top of his head. Almond eyes smiled like the Cheshire cat's through a thick beard that reached to his clavicle. Erisy was a picture of a vintage California postcard, her silken blond hair reaching the middle of her waist, her eyes bluer than the ocean itself, with a smile that could subdue an army. They were a musical duo – she sang and played guitar, and he played upright bass and offered sweet vocal harmonies. They too were on a West Coast tour, travelling by car, and they wanted to know all about my experiences. Raff owned a bike store in Santa Barbara, so his enthusiasm for my adventure was absolute. We didn't have long before we had to soundcheck, so, taking turns to use the bathroom, we got ready and went to Hyde Street Studios.

Hyde Street Studios is in the heart of the Tenderloin district. As I stepped out of the car, I immediately felt the history of the area – it hummed through the streets. We buzzed on the conspicuous door of the famous studio and were welcomed in by one of the engineers. Musical greatness emanated from the building. The studio we were performing in had recorded Jimi Hendrix, Earth, Wind & Fire, and Santana, just to name a few.

The concert was being held in one of their large studios, and as more musicians and audience members gathered, the energy in the room grew. The audience sat on the carpeted floor, and each band took a turn and played their songs acoustically. It was a beautiful event, intimate and rustic, drawing the audience into the heart of the music.

I had promised myself that I'd sing my new song, 'Road Trip'. Closing my eyes, and hoping I'd remember the lyrics, I told this room of strangers my story through song. It was met with rapturous applause.

'Thank you,' I said. 'I want to play another original, but before I do, is anyone, by any chance, driving to Half Moon Bay tomorrow morning? I kinda need a ride,' I asked the audience, half in jest and not expecting any reaction other than possible laughter. To my surprise, a young, scrappy-looking guy named Mike who worked at the studio raised his hand. 'I am,' he called out.

It turned out that he hadn't, in fact, planned to drive to Half Moon Bay but he did have the morning off, which seemed like the next best thing, so we made a deal. I would get the coffee and muffins, and he would drive me south and deliver me to the point I had reached yesterday by bike and continue my journey. That way I wouldn't be cheating or failing at all. In fact, I felt I was winning at last – and I knew I couldn't have done so without the generous help of strangers, now friends.

Jeremy and his young son were at the show. When we said farewell, we both knew it would be for the last time. He had his life and I had mine. He kissed me hard on the mouth, his son cringing at his dad's open show of affection, and then they left.

Erisy and Raff were driving all the way to Santa Barbara that night.

'Dude, you should totally stay with us when you get to Santa Barbara,' Raff offered.

'Yeah, it'd be great to see you when you get there,' Erisy added. 'Maybe we could do a show or something?'

'Totally,' Raff went on. 'It'll be rad to see you and hear your new stories. Let us know if you need anything in the meantime. I can put you in touch with some folks along the way if you need any friends.'

I waved them off in their silver Subaru and headed back to Dean's place. Dean and I said goodbye that night, as I would be leaving before dawn and he pleaded with me not to wake him.

In the morning, Mike pulled up outside the apartment in a rusted Toyota. I hadn't known how small Mike's car was when we'd made the plan the previous evening, and now I wasn't so sure this would work after all. There was a look of doubt on Mike's face too when he saw the amount of gear I had, but still he insisted it would all fit.

Together we dismantled and squeezed my bike, in many pieces, into the backseat of his car, oil from my chain smearing across his already filthy seat covers. My panniers squeezed into the trunk and front seat. Miraculously, the doors closed.

We drove fast down the highway, the windows wide open, rock music blaring from the tape player, sipping on coffee and eating breakfast muffins. We got to Half Moon Bay in an effortless hour. Before I put my bike back together, we jumped in the ocean for a swim. Mike was as happy to go to Half Moon Bay as I was grateful to him for the ride.

'Good luck with everything!' I said, throwing my arms around his skinny frame in a hug. 'And thanks! You saved my bacon.'

After reassembling my bike, I got on and rode away.
It was like slipping into a pair of comfortable pyjamas. I
was once again a lone bird travelling south and, no matter
what, I would continue my journey to where the air was
warmer.

17

FAST-FORWARD

HALF MOON BAY – SANTA CRUZ – CARMEL-BY-THE-SEA:
190 KILOMETRES

Tailwinds are a gift from the gods. It is not until you experience a headwind that you understand how the slightest breeze can change your whole outlook on life. A tailwind has just as much authority to alter your mood, but instead of sapping all your energy it is like an injection of superhuman power.

As I continued south towards Santa Cruz, the wind was like the gentle but forceful hand of a mother guiding her child, pushing me along on the flat at an effortless 51 kilometres per hour. I even climbed hills at 45 kilometres per hour, and descended at wheel-quivering, heart-racing speeds of over 70 kilometres per hour. I was flying.

The fog cleared, and the sun shone down blissfully upon the world, lifting endless shades of blue from the surface of the ocean. As far as I could tell, I was the only cyclist on the road, and I was enjoying the feeling of being queen of the road. I stopped for a moment to shed some layers of clothing, and as I was doing so I turned to see a gaggle of cycle tourists peddling steadily towards me. I quickly stuffed my extra clothing into my front panniers, got back on my bike and sped onward, trying to maintain my autonomous road space. From afar, the group looked like a family of all ages. They were taking up a fair chunk of the shoulder, and the last thing I wanted was to get stuck behind them. I stood on my pedals and set off at a sprint, trying to put as much distance between them and me as I could. Soon they were out of sight and I slowed my pace again.

Not 200 metres offshore, a humpback whale breached, revealing its striated belly, before landing with an almighty splash. I stopped and watched as she leapt out of the water again and again, waving her great tail at me, then finally disappearing under the surface. I'd forgotten about the cyclists I had been trying to get away from when, at that moment, they passed me by.

I saw that they were in fact four men, and every inch of their bare skin seemed to be covered in tattoos. Pots and pans, blankets and clothing hung off their bicycles, and they too were moving at quite a clip. Since we would be sharing the road after all, I pointed towards the ocean and called out, 'Whale!' They waved in acknowledgement and I began pedalling behind them. The whale swam gracefully alongside us for the next 15 kilometres.

I caught up to the group and chuckled at what a motley crew they were. Two of the cyclists looked like bona fide Vikings: they had long, matted blond hair that flowed in the wind, and large tribal tattoos on their muscular backs, arms and chest. The only detail that shattered this illusion was that they were wearing nothing but bike shoes and red speedos. This duo were travelling from Alaska to Argentina, and called themselves SpeedosWorldWide. They had recently met and teamed up with the other two cyclists, who were biking from New York to Los Angeles, sponsored by the independent chocolate company Mast Brothers.

I started chatting with Matty, a gangly but muscular redhead who wore a gentleman's moustache curled into two perfect twirls at each corner of his mouth. 'Yeah, girlfriend! I saw you changing back there,' he told me. 'We were, like, "Ooh, who's that hot chick on a bike? She's hardcore! Let's catch up to her," and then you were, like, outta there so fast with your turbo power legs. Go, girlfriend! Yeah!'

He was flamboyantly camp, and cycled with the poise and posture of a ballerina. I loved that he called me 'girlfriend' before he even knew my name. We shook gloved hands as we pedalled along, and rode side by side for the next 50 kilometres. I noticed that all four of them had matching whale tattoos on their equally matching hairy thighs.

'Yeah, we got this ink in San Francisco,' Matty told me proudly. 'Something to remember this trip, and each other, by.'

We talked all the way to Santa Cruz, and it wasn't until we were about to part ways that we realised we were neighbours in Brooklyn. Outside a McDonald's on the outskirts of Santa Cruz, we wished each other luck and tailwinds. Matty and I exchanged numbers, making a plan to celebrate our arrival in Los Angeles in just over a week.

In Santa Cruz I followed the signs to the boardwalk. I hadn't been here since I was fifteen, and I wanted to tour down memory lane. The giant sign stood tall in vivid colours, the same as it always had, only somehow it now looked much smaller.

I walked my bike through the archway and looked up at the flying gondolas, fitted with plaster passengers modelled to resemble cavemen and women. I recalled how I had, at six years old, excitedly told my mum after our visit here that I had ridden the 'flying condoms'. The Giant Dipper rattled and shook as the car raced along the tracks, the sickly-sweet smell of candy corn and corndogs impregnating the air. Having renewed my memories, I made my way to my next home away from home.

I stayed for two nights with the generous parents of my friend Julia. Once again I was given a clean bed, my own bathroom, and total comfort in which to be while I was stationed in the Santa Cruz area. I was booked for three shows that weekend. The first and last were at the Santa Cruz Coffee Roasting Co.'s stores, one in downtown and the other in Aptos, a little way along the coast. My main gig was at a wine bar called Zizzo's, in Capitola. There I joined forces with a fabulous jazz pianist, Jon Dryden, and it was a joy to collaborate musically with him.

The crowd at Zizzo's was lively, and during the break a couple dressed as 1950s darlings came up to thank us for the music. The conversation evolved to my travels and where I had stayed thus far, and I happened to mention Mill Valley.

'I grew up in Mill Valley,' the man with a classic ducktail hairdo told me.

'Really? You don't happen to know a guy called Jeremy Stone, do you?' I asked, sure the answer would be no.

'What? Yeah, we went to high school together. We've been buddies for years,' he told me.

We took a photo together and sent it to Jeremy, delighted at the way the universe seemed to spiral inwards from every direction.

As much as I enjoyed doing shows, playing music and meeting new and interesting people, the solitude of the road was calling me and I had to listen. On Friday afternoon, as soon as my coffeeshop gig was over, I decided it was time to get to Carmel-by-the-Sea. It was 86 kilometres away, but I calculated that even if I left at 3 p.m., I could be there by dark. I was imbued with a newfound fearlessness that could only have come from experience. In my weeks on the road so far I had learnt more about my own resilience and abilities that I could have imagined.

Each time I got back on my bike after more than a day of rest, a surge of elation flowed through my every cell. To me, the definition of freedom was to click my bags onto my pannier rack, my shoes into my pedals, and go. I had proved to myself that what I was doing was possible, and I was able to achieve more than I had trusted myself to before. I had overcome the hardest physical trials that I had experienced in my life, and not only was I still smiling, I was actually thriving on the adventure and challenge. Balancing my heavy bike was now second nature to me, and riding for six or more hours a day felt like little more than a walk in the park. My body was strong, my lungs as hardworking and efficient as a ship's bellows, and my mind as clear as a mountain lake. Any desire to rest and spend time in one place had all but disappeared. I was becoming addicted to the endorphins and adrenaline of the road. When I needed that high, I knew exactly how to get it.

Before I left Santa Cruz, I made a phone call. The phone rang until it cut off with a monotone beep. I dialled again, and this time a loud, gruff, sing-song voice answered: 'What, what, bris bonny ho, is that the pigeon carrier I've been awaiting?'

'Um, hello…Is that Scot?' I inquired nervously.

''Tis he, 'tis I – who so should wish to know?' he responded, Shakespearean in his tone.

'Hello, Scot, it's Jo Wallfisch here. I hope this is a good time to call? I wanted to see if it would be okay if I arrived a day earlier than planned – I was thinking to leave Santa Cruz this afternoon.'

'Gosh golly, truly and well. As the whipper-snatcher said to the owl at sea, keep your barrel oiled and the winds at yer back. What time will you be reaching Bad Manors?' said the voice on the end of the line.

'I think I'll arrive by seven. That's my hope, anyway – before it gets dark.'

'Very well. I'll leave the back door open,' he said. 'If I'm asleep, be sure to wake me and we can share a beer to celebrate.' And with that he hung up.

This was Scot Macbeth, with whom I'd be staying in Carmel. I had never met him in person, though I had heard his name before. He was an older gentleman and friend of the Carmel Bach Festival, and he knew my mother well. I was buoyed by the theatricality of our phone exchange and travelled on.

Heading out of Santa Cruz, I kept mostly to small roads and cycle paths, cutting a wide arc on the map to avoid the highway. I didn't mind the extra miles, which took me through the placid farmlands. The air was filled with the pungent stench of warm cabbage and artichoke, and a thousand shades of green lit up like shining cats' eyes in the late-afternoon sunlight. Through the waving sprinklers beautiful rainbows bowed, stretching from the dark soil to the light sky. I hadn't passed a soul all afternoon, but for a few farm workers silhouetted in the distance across the fields, when I heard what sounded like a swarm of bees approaching.

I looked back to see three road cyclists speeding towards me in garish jerseys on featherlight bikes. The race was on, so I pushed hard on my pedals and increased my speed a little, but it was no use. They whizzed past me, creating a breeze in their wake, and I nodded hello as they went by.

At a crossroad a few hundred metres ahead, they stopped. When I caught up with them I put on my most nonchalant smile and said, 'Hello!' They were ripping open protein bars and glucose gels with their teeth like ravenous hounds, and at first only grunted in response.

Then one cyclist took his bar from his mouth in an attempt to be polite, and said, 'Hello.'

'You're carrying a lot of luggage there,' commented another, pointing towards my gear. 'Where have you come from?'

'I biked from Portland, but today just Santa Cruz,' I answered.

'What have you got in there? Rocks?' the third man piped up, laughing at his own humour.

'Gold bricks, actually. Where are you guys riding today?'

'Oh, just San Francisco to Monterey,' the laughing man answered, and took another bite of power bar.

'In one day?' I asked, impressed but trying not to show it.

'Yeah, it's a long ride, but we're almost there,' the pointing man said. He had the map on his handlebars, and he also seemed to be the one supplying the edible energy, so I gathered he was the leader of the pack.

'Have you been camping the whole way down the coast?' the most tired of the three asked.

'No, I've only camped twice,' I admitted, 'but I've been lugging my tent the whole way in case I need it.'

'Wow! You must be hauling – what, twenty KGs?' said the leader.

'More like thirty-five,' I shrugged. 'How heavy are those bikes?' I pointed back, and in unison they laughed.

'About eight pounds, maybe a little more with water bottles,' the pointer told me. He rolled his bike towards me and challenged me to lift it.

With only my index finger, I lifted his shining white bike clear off the ground.

'Okay, who wants to try and lift my bike, then?' I challenged, and the three men snorted, 'No, thank you!'

'Well, fellas, it's time we were off,' the leader instructed. 'We've still got a ways to go. Good luck to you!' he said to me, and they clipped in.

'Good luck to you also,' I replied, and waved as they rode away in their rainbow uniforms. I watched them for a second, and then decided to chase them down. I wasn't prepared to eat their dust that easy. Hauling my energy, I caught up with them and passed by with a subtle shake of my behind, but just as my lungs were telling me to stop I came to an intersection and didn't know which way to turn. I looked back – the three musketeers were now just metres away. I tried to make a quick decision but it was too late.

'Are you lost?' asked the pointer, smiling.

'No, I'm just trying to decide whether to take the back route or the highway,' I told him.

'We're taking the highway. It's not so bad from here. The other route is way too long,' said the leader. 'Have fun!' he called as they set off again, this time at a pace I could never match.

I watched as they headed down the straight road towards the highway and decided I would follow. Knowing there were other cyclists ahead of me felt reassuring, in that they would prepare the cars to be aware of me and my safety in their wake. Besides, that was the direction the sun was setting, and I wanted to ride into it.

Fatigue didn't hit me until Fort Ord Dunes State Park, near Monterey. The evening was drawing in fast. The sand dunes glowed pink and the ocean glistened mesmerically as it absorbed every shade of the sunset, reflecting it back with diamond complexity. I had ridden this path ten years earlier on a day trip, and as I drew nearer to Carmel-by-the-Sea everything felt familiar. Ahead was the Monterey Bay Aquarium, and soon bright-yellow fun bikes joined me on the cycle path. The wind had died down, neither pushing me forward nor holding me back, and I was chasing the light.

Weaving through downtown Monterey, I followed my nose back to Highway 1. I didn't have to look at my map, the years spent driving these streets with my mum still embossed on my mind. Eventually I crested a hill and saw the green sign that had always thrilled me when I was a child, pointing to Ocean Avenue.

The day had made way for the gloaming, and everything was illuminated by its own light, a strange neon glow that almost seemed to emanate from within. I swooped into the quaint town of Carmel-by-the-Sea and breathed in the familiar scent of warm tarmac, salt air, cypress, pine and eucalyptus. The unlit streets were now completely dark. Slowly, my eyes adjusted to the black and I followed the sound of the ocean, down Tenth Avenue towards Scenic Road and Carmel Beach.

Through the cypress trees, I could see the Pacific shining in the moonlight. The long, pristine stretch of beach was punctuated by a few campfires, which glowed like rubies. The stars were coming out from their hiding places, and soon thereafter I arrived.

18

PRAYER FLAGS

Around a modest stone bungalow, more than a hundred multicoloured Buddhist prayer flags waved in the sea breeze. Strung from every corner, zigzagging from the garden fence to the roof and back again, these symbols of hope, peace, gratitude and love welcomed me. I pushed my bike across the gravel driveway and tried the back door; as Scot had promised, it was open.

I entered a large, chaotic garage and found a corner to leave my bike. Through a second door I walked into a small, dimly lit room that smelled of old papers and wool. Piled high in leaning towers were dozens of books. Books of photographs of the Himalayas and stories of heroic mountain climbers, scores of Mozart, Bach and Beethoven, poetry by Edward Lear, Hilaire Belloc and Dr Seuss, tomes by Proust and children's books by Roald Dahl grew from the floor like stalagmites in a cave. Every space on every shelf was taken up by porcelain miniatures, antique lamps, stuffed toy animals that were missing eyes or limbs, and books upon books upon books. A radio, tuned in between stations, played an eerie mix of static and classical music.

There was no sign of Scot, but beyond the kitchen I heard more music. I trod carefully through the small and cluttered kitchen and into the main living room. Following the sound of the quiet orchestra, I was led towards a light coming from a room in the corner of the house. As I got closer, I could hear deep, earth-trembling snoring rise above the music. I peered around the doorframe into a brightly lit stone room, a single fluorescent strip light glowing on the low ceiling. Lying on top of the bed in a green sleeping bag, his mouth wide open, his eyes half-closed, was Scot Macbeth. He looked like the caterpillar from *Alice in Wonderland*.

I had tried to make no sound as I didn't want to wake him, but he sensed my presence. With a jolt he sat up in bed and called out, 'Who goes there? Is that she who arrived on the will of the wind and the bally-ho beat of the drum?' He looked over his shoulder to where I stood frozen in the doorway, and caught me with his glassy blue eyes.

'Hi, Scot,' I said. 'I'm so sorry if I startled you.'

'Not at all, not at all! I am glad you woke me.' Then, as if to himself, 'I often wonder if I'll wake up at all these days.' Looking back to me, in an emboldened tone he said, 'Come, come, let's have that beer.'

He unzipped his sleeping bag, stepped into his slippers and tottered towards me in his striped pyjamas. Scot was eighty-seven years old but had the energy and mental spryness of a young man. I followed him to the kitchen, slightly embarrassed that I had caught him in his pyjamas, but he seemed neither coy nor self-conscious. He opened the fridge and pulled out two tins of lager, and then led me back to the room of curiosities.

'So, you like an adventure, do you?' he said with a twinkle in his eye. 'I too have had my share of adventure. I spent half my life living in the Himalayan mountains, you know. I was part of one of the first teams to attempt Mount Everest.' His grandiloquence convincing and charming, I smiled. He gestured to the books on the floor. 'I'm glad you are visiting. It's always good to be in the company of a fellow crusader.'

We passed the rest of the evening sipping beers and talking of adventure. Scot had a marvellous mind, pulling quotes from nonsense verse and prose, woven in with true tales of his life in the mountains. After a while, and with the beer taking effect, the conversation took on a surreal edge and finally we said goodnight. I made my nest on the small, horsehair chaise longue beneath a large bookshelf. Despite my exhaustion, I didn't sleep well, waking often to turn in my sleeping bag and sneezing from the dust in the room.

I was glad when the sky grew light again and I could head out for an early swim in the ocean. I had gifted myself an extra day in Carmel by arriving the previous night, and I spent it mostly alone with the waves on the beach. I didn't need any other conversation than that of the ebb and flow of the tide, the seagulls lifting and landing, and the sky turning from white to blue to pink to black. I wandered home in the late evening, tired and ready for a better night's rest. The following morning I was booked to sing at the Unitarian Church in Pebble Beach, so I really wanted my beauty sleep.

When I opened the garage door, the radio blasted at full volume, tuned to a major classical work. Scot was sitting in a rocking chair with his eyes closed, hands resting on his lap, humming along to the music. Again I did not not want to disturb his reverie, but as soon as I crept through the door his eyes shot open and he threw his hands in the air.

'Brilliant! I'm glad you're back. I've been waiting to crack open the Lagavulin all evening.'

We sat in the kitchen, the bare strip light above us buzzing like a lost bee. Scot perched himself on the stepladder-cum-stool, and I sat on the small step between rooms, my back against the doorframe. He poured me a heavy dram and microwaved two foil packets of vegetarian curry, the kind you would take on a mountaineering trip. We ate from plastic bowls with metal spoons, and drank single-malt whisky until past midnight, continuing our nonsensical conversation from the previous evening. Scot was a treasure-trove of wisdom and I eagerly soaked it up. Our faces flushed, and our words slipperier than drunken fish, we bade each other goodnight.

I was glad for the alcohol streaming through my veins, hoping that, no matter how uncomfortable my bed might be, the whisky would knock me out until the morning. I brushed my teeth, put on my makeshift pyjamas and slid open the french windows that led to the back garden and, just beyond, the ocean. The small and eccentrically cluttered room was instantly transformed by the effervescence of the outside world.

I zipped myself into my sleeping bag, turned off the lamp at my feet and closed my heavy eyes. I listened to the meditative lapping of the waves until they melted into my subconscious and the great silence of sleep washed over me.

Bang! Crash! I was awoken abruptly. My heart thumped at my sternum wall, my face tingled and the hairs in my ears stood on end. I didn't dare open my eyes. From somewhere in the room came the sound of a heavy object falling off a shelf and breaking.

I waited a couple more seconds before cracking my eyes open just enough to see my surroundings. As far as I could see, nothing had in fact moved. I opened my eyes a little wider, slowly turned my head and scanned the whole room. Everything was in its place.

It must be in the garage, I thought, and looked towards the door. It was ajar. Whatever had made that noise was in the garage, and the door was not closed.

I pushed my sleeping bag down over my legs without unzipping it and, as quietly as I could, tiptoed to the door. As soon as I was within arm's reach I pushed it closed and locked the latch. I looked around the room once more, my ears ringing with the silence and the sound of my racing heart. Sure that it was probably one of the many poorly balanced objects in the garage finally succumbing to gravity, I went back to my nest. I slowed my breath with some meditative exhalations, and eventually found my way back to sleep.

Scrape! Bang! Smash!

I scrunched my eyes tight. This time the phantom sound came from right above my head. I slid down into my sleeping bag until my face was covered, listening as I hid. Something was in the room with me! I willed my heart to beat more quietly.

Rustle! Crash! It was near, and getting nearer.

I decided I wasn't going to be caught out by whatever was causing this cacophony, and counted to three under my breath. I pulled my sleeping bag down from my face and opened my eyes. The glow of the moon cast strange shadows across the piles of books and statues on the floor of the dark room. I sat up, my feet tucked beneath me, and looked around. Nothing was out of place. Not one artefact had fallen or shifted. The garage door was still locked, and the door to the kitchen was closed tight.

Feeling braver, I reached for my phone and shone the torch around the room. Nothing. I switched on the lamp at the foot of the bed, and suddenly the shadows disappeared and the room was thrown into a golden glow, everything as still and friendly as before. My mouth was dry from fear. Gingerly I walked across the room in my bare feet and opened the door to the kitchen. The buzzing strip light was still aglow. I filled a plastic cup with water from the tap and gulped.

As I turned to walk back into the music room, my heart stopped. The back doors leading outside were wide open. Scanning the room one more time to make sure nobody was hiding, I walked briskly to the doors, pulled them closed and drew the curtains. *Whatever was in here must have gone out*, I reassured myself.

I retreated once more to my narrow bed, switched off the light and closed my eyes. Sleep was nowhere to be found. I looked at my phone: 2 a.m. I had to be up in five hours, and the distraction of fear now turned into frustration. I had hoped to get a good rest before my concert but my chance was dwindling by the minute. I took some long, slow breaths and tried to find a restful state. Finally, my body twitched microscopically, my eyelids sagged and I fell between the conscious and subconscious worlds.

Whoosh!

A breeze across my face woke me, but there was no airflow in the room, every door and window firmly sealed. Something had brushed across my face and I was ready to fight. I opened my eyes, turned my phone torch on and swept the room with its beam.

Then I saw it. At the foot of my bed, perched on the globe of the lamp – eyes gleaming, ears twitching, whiskers flickering, a foot of thick pink tail curled around the bronze figurine holding up the bulb – was a giant rat. He stared at me unblinking as I blinded him with the torchlight. I sat frozen as the rat cleaned its face with its sharp-clawed paws. It sniffed at the air, the edges of its ragged ears rotating at the smallest sound.

The rat and I stared at one another. It was impossible to tell who was more afraid. He leaned towards me, his tiny claws reaching out as if ready to leap, so I sat up taller. As soon as I moved, the rat disappeared. It moved with imperceptible speed, so fast that I couldn't tell which direction it had gone – but wherever it was, it was still in there with me. I walked to the back doors and opened them wide, then took my sleeping bag and pillow and vacated the room. The rat could have it.

By now it was 4 a.m. and the hours were slipping by on fast-forward, the crest of dawn already lighting the sky. I spent the last two hours of the night on the sofa in Scot's living room, and woke, disorientated and disgruntled just after six. Scot walked right past me in his pyjamas and started shuffling through papers on his desk. I hoped he hadn't noticed me but, without looking over, he said, 'What are you doing there?'

'Good morning,' I yawned. 'It's a bit of a long story, but there was a rat in my room last night.'

'A rat? Gosh, how could he have got in there?'

The afternoon before I left Carmel, Scot had asked me to do some errands for him, such as go to the grocery store and fill his car with gas. I was glad to oblige, and took his Subaru to the Safeway at Cross Roads Shopping Center. Scot's shopping list included bananas, kimchi and microwavable curry packets. I also stocked up on supplies for my onward journey to Big Sur – dried fruit, protein bars, a block of cheese and some fresh fruit – then I drove home.

Scot's cottage was situated on the corner of a twisty, narrow road on the very edge of Carmel. In general there was hardly any footfall from passers-by, and barely any traffic. It was a quiet corner off the beaten track; the only reason to drive that way might be to dine at Clint Eastwood's Mission Ranch Inn across the street. I could see the colourful prayer flags waving in the breeze as I rounded the corner and came to a stop. Blocking my path, walking slowly in black jeans, black plimsoll shoes, a black denim jacket and black sunglasses, was the stranger from Half Moon Bay.

This was the third time I had seen him – first just south of San Francisco, then at Half Moon Bay, and now three days and 250 kilometres south in Carmel-by-the-Sea. Although it was irrational, I had the strong sensation that he had something to tell me.

I pulled into Scot's gravel driveway, turned off the engine and stepped out of the car. Crossing the street in my bare feet, the tarmac warm against my soles, I stood in front of him, stopping his slow passage, and asked, 'Who are you?'

He lifted his left hand to his sunglasses and removed them, revealing sapphire-blue eyes. He held out his right hand and shook mine. He told me his name, his voice soft, then asked for mine. I told him, 'Jo.' He looked up to the sky and repeated it back to me as if it were a word he'd never heard before.

'I've seen you before,' I said. 'Just south of San Francisco, and then again at Half Moon Bay. How did you get here?' I was stumbling over my words.

'I walked,' he told me simply. After a brief pause, he continued: 'I woke up in my shitty apartment in San Francisco about ten days ago, left my keys behind and started walking.' His eyes shimmered as he smiled at me. 'What about you?'

'I biked here. I'm making my way from Portland to LA,'

I told him, the repetition of this phrase beginning to sound strange.

'That's very impressive,' he said, his words slow and somehow faraway.

I assured him that my trip was easy compared to walking with no plan, but maybe I was wrong. Maybe his route was truly free, and I was complicating things with all my planning.

We stood there for what felt like an eternity, two lone travellers with one common truth: we were both going south. We hugged at the edge of Carmel as the sun beat down on us. It was the same sun that would follow us as we continued alone, alongside to the same ocean that would always be to our right, beneath the same moon.

At last we said, 'Goodbye, and good luck,' and I watched as he walked on and disappeared from my view forever.

19

BIG SUR

CARMEL-BY-THE-SEA – KIRK CREEK: 89 KILOMETRES

'Keep your barrel oiled and your powder dry!' Scot said, and he handed me a yellow prayer flag. 'The road is waiting, you'd better go!' I thanked him again and saddled up. 'Think fast, but live slow,' Scot called after me as I pedalled away, and I waved until I was around the corner and out of sight.

Despite the rat, the dust and the whisky hangover, the days I'd spent with him had been precious. He was the most unique and genuine person I could have hoped to meet, and through his riddles and rhymes he transfused a wisdom that would remain with me. With the spirit of the road running through my veins, I was ready for the most anticipated part of my journey yet: Big Sur.

The raging wildfires that for several weeks had ravaged the coastal hills from Big Sur to San Simeon had finally been subdued, and the Pacific Coast Highway had been reopened just two days before my departure from Carmel. I was anticipating riding through thick smoke and had secretly promised myself that if the air seemed dangerous for my health, I would turn back and either stay another day in Carmel or get a ride through the worst affected areas.

Carmel was sucked in with fog the morning I left, but the layer of cloud glowed bright with the promise that the sun would burn through long before noon. Passing the ancient Carmel Mission Basilica on Rio Road, I sped towards the Crossroads Shopping Center, stopping at the intersection where the highway sliced through Carmel. To my right was the sign I had been waiting for:

> ## BIG SUR 26 miles
> ## SAN LUIS OBISPO 132 miles
> ## LOS ANGELES 337 miles

This was the first time I'd seen a road sign to Los Angeles; from here on, every sign would mark the miles of my ever quickening approach to LA.

The hard shoulder was dusted with sand blown over from the beaches, revealing the tyre marks of cyclists who had gone before me. Pushing down on my pedals, the only way was south. I passed Point Lobos, with its turquoise-blue waters, cheeky chipmunks and parliament of magpies, Tickle Pink Inn and the cragged cypress trees that clung to the rocks on the low coastline, and Spindrift Road, with its memories of my first teenage crush. Then I left Carmel behind me.

The road seemed to narrow as it turned inland, away from the steely ocean, and short, fragrant trees began to close in on both sides of the road. The air changed from salty to sweet, but it was not just the scent of wildflowers or even of the pines scattered on the dusty earth. It was a distinct and ominous smell, reminiscent of an old campfire, a smell that clings to the back of your throat and stings your eyes. Instead of the black smoke that I had feared would be filling the air, there was just a haze of sunset pink covering everything, as though I was wearing rose-tinted glasses.

Breathing through my nose, I tried to avoid inhaling the delicate soot that remained in the air, but the microscopic particles went everywhere – in my eyes, on my skin, into my pores, swallowed down with my saliva – and I could feel my lungs tensing. I wrapped my scarf around my mouth and nose and breathed through the condensation of my breath.

The fog had dissipated now and I was enjoying the sunshine's warmth on my skin – the same summer heat that had wreaked deadly havoc across the dry grasses of this land just a week earlier. I progressed along the road cautiously, keeping my eyes open for any sign of fire, but there was none. I picked up my pace and got into a strong rhythm, riding at 25 kilometres per hour without much effort at all.

Soon the road opened out again and began to incline, stalling my efforts and making my luggage feel like lead. Ahead was the Big Sur Bakery and the Big Sur Post Office, the first markers that I was now officially in Big Sur territory. I pushed forward with all my effort, standing on the pedals and heaving on the handlebars until I came to a complete stop, toppling off in a sweaty mess outside the post office. This was my last chance to make my life easier and get rid of some luggage.

I leaned my bike against a wooden fence and started to unpack my panniers, placing my loop pedal, tent, clothing, pots, pans and anything else I wouldn't need for the next ten days on the ground around me. Just then a police officer rode up on his motorbike and parked next to me.

He took off his helmet, stepped purposefully off of his large motorcycle and looked at me from behind his dark glasses for longer than I was comfortable with. His expression was so serious and intimidating that I was sure he was going to tell me that I couldn't ride my bike through Big Sur, or fine me for making a mess here in the parking lot. But he broke into a smile, raised his eyebrows above his sunglasses and said, 'Nice bike! You got quite a load there!' Before I could respond, he walked into the post office, chuckling to himself.

'Thanks,' I said to his back, and shrugged.

I took armfuls of excess luggage into the post office and laid it on the counter. The clerk gave me a strange look, then handed me a large box. 'Where is this going?' he asked.

'Back to New York,' I said, hurriedly stuffing everything in, including the outer shell of my tent, pegs and pole.

Sending my tent home had been a major source of debate between Scot and me. I wanted to get rid of it completely, as I'd only used it twice in three weeks and didn't foresee a time I would need it again – except for a single night in Big Sur. While he understood my desire to lighten my load, he had disagreed. 'If you have to be without anything in the wild,' he said, 'you never want to be without shelter!'

With his words running through my mind, I had decided to keep *most* of my tent. That is to say, I packed the waterproof outer shell and all the hardware into the box, keeping only the inner shell and ground sheet. I also kept my sleeping bag. I would prop the tent up with my pannier bags, I resolved, creating a shelter similar to a bivvy bag. If I could accept one slightly uncomfortable and possibly damp night's sleep under the stars, I would have so much more freedom and speed without all that extra weight on my bike. I was happy with that, and sent my gear packing back east.

With my panniers almost 9 kilograms lighter, the hill ahead did not seem so steep after all. Sweat poured down my face, dripping off the end of my nose and onto my phone, which was attached to my handlebars. I had started to love climbs like this, which filled me with a feeling of invincibility and pure strength.

The air was dry and the sweet smell of smoke seemed to clear as the road neared the ocean again. The heart of Pfeiffer State Park brought me in contact with crowds of tourists driving their rental cars and RVs, but also the promise of ice creams, sodas and imminent views of the big blue. After a gruelling but satisfying climb, I reached the top of the first major hill of the day, and from there careened down towards Nepenthe Phoenix restaurant, where I stopped for lunch.

I locked my bike on a lamppost in the crammed parking lot of Nepenthe, just beneath the wooden carving of a phoenix that presided proudly over the establishment. Clicking across the car park in nothing but my lycra shorts, a sweat-soaked sports bra and my filthy cycling gloves, I was quite conspicuous alongside couples in well-ironed white chinos and pressed pastel blouses. They looked at me as though I were from outer space – and I smiled back at them, thinking much the same.

I ate my snacks on the deck, looking out over the great cliffs that dropped to the ocean, slurping happily on a root beer with a maraschino cherry on top. Then I caught sight of the smoke. A giant plume of billowing black smoke rose above the hills to the east. I pointed in alarm, but those who also saw it didn't seem concerned. Two helicopters rose up from the ocean carrying buckets of ocean water, and disappeared over the hill. A woman sitting next to me could see the concern in my face, and reassured me that this smoke was from a controlled fire: they were back-burning the hills, trying to prevent further disaster. I felt relieved, but also shocked at the reality of how devastating the original fires must have been.

Fatigue was starting to set in as I relaxed on the warm deck at Nepenthe, so I knew it was time to push on. My destination was Kirk Creek Campground, about 40 kilometres further south. As soon as my wheels exited the parking lot, gravity sucked me, as if down a flume, onto the narrow, steep highway, which curved suddenly to the right at a 90-degree angle. Adrenaline surged through me and I was fully alert again. I saw the Henry Miller Memorial Library on my left, but now that I was back on the road I was reluctant to stop. Just as I was about to pass it by, I flicked my eyes behind me to check for oncoming traffic and swerved across the road and into the driveway. I wasn't in that much of a rush; what harm would it do to spend a couple of minutes brushing my hands along the bookshelves of the historical library?

The entranceway was covered with rough gravel and fallen bark, pine needles and eucalyptus leaves. I pushed my bike slowly, observing the gentle chatter and convivial scene in front me. On the sun-bathed deck of the library sat four smiling people sitting cross-legged on the warm wood, wielding coffee cups. I waved hello.

'You look like you're on quite a journey,' the skinny redhead said, pointing at my bike and smiling.

'Yep, I guess you could say that,' I replied, feeling shy.

'Would you like some coffee? Help yourself,' he gestured at the pot balanced on a low stool, then ducked into the dark doorway of the library. 'Gotta get back to work,' he said by way of farewell, leaving me alone with the other three, who continued chatting to each other as I poured myself a small cup of coffee. I sat alongside them with my legs dangling off the edge of the deck. I noticed they all had accents.

'You're Australians?' I asked, interrupting their conversation.

'Yeah, good guess!' said the tall man, his dark hair cut short against his head, his large almond eyes smiling at me.

'Where are you from?' the girl asked me, her voice as open as a sunflower, her eyes cornfield-blue.

'I'm from London, but my mum is from Melbourne, so I feel pretty Australian,' I told them.

'Nice. What brings you here?' the third answered from beneath the rim of his wide-brimmed Stetson. He had a bright-red beard that covered his freckles.

As we got talking, they told me their names: Jack, Bonnie and Jed, also known as 'JBJ'. When I told them I was Jo they instantly added me to their acronym and we became JBJJ. Our friendship sparked as quickly as flint and steel.

'Have you guys heard of Esalen?' I asked.

'We were literally just discussing that,' said Bonnie. 'We really want to go to their late-night hot springs, but we can't book it without wi-fi.'

'We're gonna drive back north to the Big Sur Bakery and book for tonight if we can,' Jed told me, hands on his hips, his bare stomach tanned from life in the sun.

'Have you ever been?' asked Jack, adjusting his Stetson so his deep-green eyes met mine.

'Yeah, a couple of times,' I said, 'and I was hoping to go tonight, but there's no way I can get back to Kirk Creek in the middle of the night on my bike.' I paused, a lightbulb going off in my mind. 'Hang on, I have a great idea,' I announced. All three turned to face me. 'Do you guys know where you're staying tonight?' I asked.

'Nah, we thought we'd just find a campsite or something,' Jed said. 'We have a camper van, so it's no biggie where we stay, really.'

'Okay, great. So why don't you guys camp at Kirk Creek – it's just 40 kilometres south of here. That's where I'm going to be camping. Then,' I paused dramatically, 'we could all go to Esalen together. If you have room in your van for me, that is.'

'Sure! Sounds good,' said Bonnie, matter-of-factly.

'Really? Amazing. So shall we meet again this evening at the campground? Oh, and would you be down to buy me a ticket for the springs if there are enough spaces available?' I asked more tentatively, unsure if they would go for that idea. 'I can pay you back tonight.'

'Sure, no worries,' said Jack. 'We can totally do that.'

They exchanged a look between them that seemed to indicate they all agreed. We hugged, and Jed spoke for all of us when he said, 'See ya later, alligator.'

I made my way to Kirk Creek not knowing for sure if I'd see JBJ again, but enthused by our meeting and their good vibes. The 40 kilometres from the Henry Miller Library to Kirk Creek were like riding a Ferris wheel, constantly rising and falling, and with the best view of the Pacific at my side. I rolled into Kirk Creek just after 6 p.m., tired to the core. I hadn't noticed JBJ pass me in their campervan and was starting to doubt if the plan was going to work after all.

As I checked in with the campsite manager, I saw Bonnie running towards me across the campsite. She had bare feet, was dressed in bathers and a baggy jumper, and was brandishing a bottle of champagne. 'Ya made it! That's so awesome! We passed you on the road earlier and waved, but we didn't wanna scare you so we didn't honk or anything,' she exclaimed, her bright Aussie accent putting a smile on every syllable. 'Besides, you looked pretty serious climbing that crazy hill back there.'

Jack and Jed were lazing in the campervan drinking cold beers when Bonnie and I appeared at the open door, arm in arm like sisters.

'Let's go swimming before the sun goes down,' I said. 'I'll just quickly set up my tent and change, and then we should go down to the water for sunset.'

The hiker-biker campsite was half-empty. I chose a spot that overlooked the cliff, so from my bed I would be able to hear and see the ocean. I laid the inner shell of my tent out on the dry ground, propping up the sides with my panniers, and smoothed out my sleeping bag before getting inside to test it out. My nose touched the mesh ceiling above me but I was cosy and felt safe. Above all, I was happy to be here in this campground, able to look at the stars while I slept. I changed out of my clothes and into my bikini, zipped up what was left of my tent and went to join JBJ.

A concealed path through an overgrown blackberry bush led us down to the ocean. We clambered down the rocky path, clinging to the champagne and some extra beers. The ocean crashed against the cliffs, spraying up liquid gold and sapphire. Jed and Bonnie fearlessly started to climb a high rock that arched in a bridge over the water. I tried to follow but the muscles in my legs were so tired that I could barely hold my weight, so I stayed with Jack and we sipped cold beer. Bonnie and Jed stripped off on top of the arch and stood with their naked bodies facing the setting sun, creating two perfect silhouettes atop this great bridge to the ocean. The ocean swept into the small cove where we sat with great dissonance, stirring up the heavy sand and rocks so that it was impossible to swim. I dipped my hands in and cupped the salt water, throwing it over my face, hair and arms. It was enough just to kiss the ocean.

After a dinner of beans, bread and cheese, we went for a short sleep, JBJ in their camper and me in my tiny tent. When I got there, however, it was already damp from the mist of the evening. I brushed off the largest droplets, slid into my sleeping bag and released a deep sigh of happiness. Sleep came quickly, but when I awoke at midnight I was shivering and damp. A heavy dew was settling on me and my open-to-all-elements tent was offering zero protection. I got up and followed the dim light of my head torch to JBJ's warm and dry campervan, and we drove north towards Esalen.

At 1 a.m., standing in the dark with a small group of strangers, we were rounded up by a man with a torch and a clipboard. He gave us our instructions in a monotone voice, then led the way down the steep hill towards the entrance of Esalen. I could hear the waves crashing loudly on the cliffs below.

We were led to a stone-walled changing area that offered rain showers, herbal soaps and a heated floor. Beyond the showers and through a passageway, we arrived outside, where four large bathtubs with lions' feet waited to be filled with hot, sulphurous spring water. Two large communal hot tubs clung to the cliff, with hot water that poured over the edge every time a new body entered the pool. I chose an individual bathtub and lay in the warm water for three hours, my head resting on the wide porcelain rim, my body floating weightlessly as sleep caressed my mind like a butterfly's wings. Every time I opened my eyes my vision was filled with diamonds, a million stars shining in the black of the night above.

At 4 a.m. we dressed in near silence, pulling clothes over our new skin, warmth radiating through our muscles. When we returned to Kirk Creek I bade JBJ goodnight and went back to my tiny tent. Under the dim glow of my head torch, I saw dozens of tiny rabbits' footprints all over the mesh outer-shell and my sleeping bag. The structure, or what was left of it, had been flattened by curious, muddy-footed rodents and was soaked through. I tried not to worry about it and instead turned and walked over to JBJ's campervan, where I knocked quietly on the window. Without a word Jed slid open the door and lifted up the duvet for me to crawl under. The four of us slept like baby sardines until long after the sun had dried the morning dew.

In the morning I inspected my tent more thoroughly. Luckily, I had sealed my pannier bags tightly, so no food or clothing had been taken out and strewn across the campsite. Nevertheless, I could hear Scot's gruff voice reciting Lewis Carroll's 'Jabberwocky' in a near whisper, by way of warning and I-told-you-so:

'Twas brillig, and the slithy toves
Did gyre and gamble in the wabe;
All mimsy were the borogoves,
And the mome raths outgrabe.

'If you have to be without anything in the wild,' I could hear him saying, 'you never want to be without shelter!'

JBJ were driving to Los Angeles that day. The notion that they could reach LA in a single day was futuristic to me. I was moving at the speed of the eighteenth century, before the invention of the motor, before commercial transit. I was travelling *with* the road, not just on it. Every kilometre was a conversation between body, mind, spirit and nature. I had to listen to the sky, the ground, the wind and the ocean, and decipher how I could move with them, not simply through or past them.

I was packed and ready to go before JBJ were out of their pyjamas. We had bonded and become like family overnight, and it was difficult to say goodbye.

'Make sure you stop and jump in the ocean on your way south,' I insisted before I cycled off.

'Totally,' JBJ called back in unison.

All teeth and crow's feet, Jack, Bonnie and Jed waved me goodbye, only to catch up with me twenty minutes later, flagging me down to pass me a cardigan I had left in their van. I gave them each a final hug through the windows of the campervan, and watched as they sped off down the winding coastline.

20

THE HORSE MASSEUR AND
THE TRAVELLING DOG

KIRK CREEK – MORRO BAY – SAN LUIS OBISPO:
105 KILOMETRES

The sun was high and there was not a cloud to be seen. The wind rolled in behind me, and just when I thought I had conquered the biggest challenges of Big Sur the day before, the hills that lay ahead surpassed the majesty of any climb since Oregon. A challenge greater than the climb, though, was the lack of shoulder between me and the traffic.

I had barely a wheel's breadth of space before the tarmac turned to gravel and the gravel turned to a 60-metre drop to the ocean. I wasn't going to succumb to my role as a mere cyclist and risk my life just so the view-gawking drivers could speed to their next photo opportunity, so I joined the traffic and defensively remained inside the thin white line. To my surprise and delight, the cars gave me a wide berth,

slowing as they approached and waving at me through
their open windows, encouraging me on as they passed.

All cars but one. With cameras pressed up to the closed
windows on both the passenger and driver sides, blocking
any reasonable line of sight for safe driving, a silver Nissan
rental brushed past me so close that its hot aluminium shell
grazed the hairs on my legs. This happened twice, and
twice I wobbled, shouted and hit the trunk as they passed
me, oblivious to the life they were playing with. In almost
1600 kilometres, this was the only driver who had ever got
too close.

Cobalt, turquoise, sapphire, azure, cyan, indigo, steel and
zaffer. Every shade of blue cascaded from the stratosphere
to the invisible depths of the Pacific and surrounded me.
Beyond the blue, the green and purple, yellow and brown
of the hills, in shadow and haze, curled back and forth to
meet the breaking waves, the soaring eagles and the ever-
changing winds.

Back in the Pure Zone, my mind was completely empty
of thought, serving only as a role of blank film upon which
to take mental pictures of the sublime beauty all around
me. My body had become an engine, working efficiently
and without complaint, recycling the energy it released,
feeding back into itself via a channel of adrenaline and
determination.

I laughed out loud as I descended the swooping hills
that took me from where the eagles soared to where I could
smell the kelp drying on the beaches. I grinned as I pulled
and pushed and heaved and grunted back up the hills
again, climbing even higher than before. It was a game and I
was winning. I wished that all the drivers could know even
a bit of what this land was offering – the gift of knowing

Big Sur with your body, of understanding the eminence of the hills, the magnitude of the land, and the spirit of the water. The knowledge that nature is not just there to look at and enjoy, to take from and keep; it is an open conversation, a revelation of how we come to live and breathe and love as we do.

In the distance I saw the road stretch out in a yawn, flattening out towards the south. I couldn't see more hills beyond and wondered if this was already the end of Big Sur. I stopped at a pullout and looked behind me at the ruffles of rock and cliff reaching back and forth into the Prussian-blue Pacific. It was almost impossible to comprehend how I had found my way here under the strength of my body alone. I never knew I could be so strong, so willing, so patient. I lifted my arms to the sky in thanks.

At that moment the wind picked up and pushed my leaning bike against my legs. I could sense that this afternoon's ride was going to be special. Before the wind changed its mind and decided to travel north instead of south, I pushed on and, like a human-powered sports car, accelerated from zero to 50 kilometres per hour in a matter of seconds. Now the cars couldn't pass me as I was riding at the speed limit, and sometimes above it. I ruled the road, and the road smiled with me.

I stopped for a moment at Elephant Seal Beach, but as soon as I turned into the parking lot I was almost blown to the ground by the same wind that had been giving me wings. I gawked at the impressive seals and then returned to pedalling, this natural gift too good not to enjoy for as long as it would last. The feeling of this tailwind was exhilarating, like a combination of jumping from a great height into a crystal-clear pool of water and making love. Freedom at its best.

I was hungry. I had disappeared into such a deep state of meditation and athletic focus that I hadn't noticed the minutes turning to hours over the last 50 kilometres. I had ridden for almost four hours without stopping, and my hands shook as my glycemic levels plummeted, my system saturated with adrenaline and lactic acid. I was high as a kite and running on empty.

As I pulled into Ragged Point, I realised that this was the end of Big Sur. I had done it. Just like that. I pulled my bike past the picnic tables and leaned it against the window of the cafeteria. I stepped into the cavernous canteen and waited for anyone who resembled a server to appear. I noticed rootbeer on offer in the soda fountain, and as my hunger levels rose I became grumpy and impatient. Pacing stiffly up and down the empty cafe, looking for any sign of life, I noticed a man lingering around my bicycle outside. I watched him as he walked by and entered the canteen.

'Is that your bike?' he asked me, his accent tinged with a sweet southern drawl, his face ruddy red, his hair silkworm-white.

'Yeah, it is actually,' I replied, more defensively than I had meant.

'You're on a big trip, I see. Did you just bike through Big Sur this morning?' He was smiling, his red cheeks shining.

I smiled back and lowered my head as if to say, 'It was nothing.'

'Are you waiting for someone here?' he asked.

'Yes – is the restaurant even open? I'm starving!'

'Oh, sure it is. Give me a minute, I'll find someone for

you.' He disappeared behind the counter and I wondered if he might own the place. Shortly he returned, and towering behind him was the person I was waiting for. I ordered a rootbeer and a cheese sandwich with fries, thanked the stranger and walked outside. He followed.

'My name is Gary – Gary White,' he said as he walked towards me. 'I've been on my fair share on bike tours myself.'

He wore heavy denim jeans and black leather boots. Under his arm was a white felt Stetson, his denim collar cinched closed with a silver bolo tie. As I stretched and waited for my lunch, he kept talking. 'Back in 1988 I did a land race across America with Bob Weiland, a double amputee who walked across America on his arms. The two of us crossed the country in thirty-four days on a three-wheeler trike.'

I could see flashes of vivid memory glimmering across his eyes. I listened, trying to absorb the magnitude of this tale.

He changed the subject. 'Your shoulders must be tight after hauling all that weight through Big Sur. Would you like a massage?'

I recoiled, and as politely as I could declined and tried to change the subject again. My cheese sandwich had still not arrived, and the rootbeer had barely eased the hunger that ran through me.

'I apologise,' he said. 'I didn't explain. I'm a qualified equine masseur – a two-time award winner, in fact. I would be more than happy to help release the tension in your back and shoulders before you travel on today.'

I was not convinced. 'I'll have a think about it,' I said. 'I really must eat something first,' and I stood to check on my sandwich. Gary left me in peace and I ate on a picnic table beneath a blue parasol. My hands gradually stopped shaking and soon I felt better.

Just as I was about to leave, Gary reappeared. 'Are you sure you don't want a massage? You're safe with me. I promise to be respectful, and I promise you will feel stronger than ever afterwards.'

I gave in and accepted. It wasn't until he touched my shoulders that I realised how much pain I was in. I had grown so used to the sensation that, as long as it didn't hinder my biking, I took no notice anymore. I lay face-down on the picnic table and yielded to this horse masseur as he unpicked every ropy muscle in my back. My spine cracked and popped, my pelvis crunched as my hips fell back into alignment, and my neck cried out in pain and then surrendered in silence.

Gary sat me up and continued to work on my arms and legs. 'Horses are the best teachers,' he said as he worked, and after a while he announced he was done.

I was jelly, but when I stood I felt ten inches taller. 'Thank you so much, Gary. Can I buy you lunch?'

'Nope,' he said, 'you don't owe me a thing. I'm just happy to know I could help you on your way. You're doing something quite unique here.'

He was another gift from the road, given without expectation. He placed his Stetson in the pannier of his motorbike and replaced it with his helmet. I, too, got on my bike, and we said goodbye, his business card tucked into my handlebar bag.

I awoke the next morning lying diagonally across a king-size bed, my face buried in marshmallow-soft pillows, the duvet pulled up to my nose, my hair strewn in all directions. My sunburnt skin felt like sandpaper against the silky sheets, and as I gathered consciousness, the weight of my exhaustion sank my body heavily into the soft mattress.

Moving only my eyes, I took in the motel room. The textured stucco walls were painted beige and stopped short at the low ceiling. The worn dark-blue carpet enhanced the cave effect, as slivers of watery sunlight fell in through the slatted vertical blinds. Glancing at my phone, I saw that it was already 10 a.m. I had been asleep for almost twelve hours.

I threw off the duvet and slid to the edge of the bed nearest the window, then sat up, assessing each ache and strain in my back and legs. As I stood, my thighs felt lethargic and not entirely my own. When I tried to stretch my quads, the sunburn screamed as I pulled my skin taut. I had run out of sunblock in Carmel and had rationalised that my skin was probably tanned enough by now that I wouldn't get too sunburnt anymore, and that my legs would be the least affected. I was wrong. Instead, I had developed a striking three-tiered suntan/burn that resembled a Dulux paint colour chart, each shade divided by a perfectly straight line. The lines on my left thigh were higher than those on my right, as my shorts had shifted unevenly as I biked.

I stood naked in front of the bathroom mirror and examined my asymmetrical tan, giggling to myself. I hadn't seen my body in a full-length mirror for weeks, and I looked different now. The muscles in my legs, arms, abdomen and hips were more defined, cutting shadows around my more pronounced ribs and pelvis bones. Even my face seemed different. I looked more relaxed and open, the tension of the city having dissolved. The tips of my auburn hair were white-blond, and upon my nose and cheeks were new tiny freckles.

I walked barefoot to the papery blinds and peered through. Across the deck and above the buildings below I could see the top of the impressive rock of Morro Bay, my first port of call after Big Sur.

I had rolled in the previous evening and bypassed the magnificent rock, a watercolour washed in sunset. I'd been longing to go swimming in the ocean beneath its vast shadow, but I couldn't fathom the energy. Neither did I stop to check out the beach campsite, though I saw a handful of tents nestled in the sands, and envied the sleep their inhabitants would have, lulled by the ocean's roar. My roofless tent would simply not hold up to another night. I followed the quaint main street of Morro Bay until I saw a strip of motels and put my credit card down on the first one with a vacancy sign. I lay down on the king-size bed, closed my eyes and, as though I were clicking through the slides of a View-Master, relived the experiences of the previous two days riding through the heart of Big Sur, until sleep drew the curtain closed.

The late start didn't matter much, as my agenda for the day was undemanding: find breakfast, suss out a warm patch of sand on which to lie, then bike a leisurely 20 kilometres to San Luis Obispo. This was a rest day.

I went downstairs to the motel dining-room-cum-windowless-storeroom and found breakfast. The room was filled with plastic tables and chairs, upon which one could eat plastic toast and spread plastic jam with a plastic knife, and drink plastic orangeade served from a plastic spout, accompanied by plastic instant coffee sipped from melting plastic cups. I can't say that I skipped breakfast, though I tried to forget it quickly.

The rock of Morro Bay stood stark against the endless blue sky. The waves rose and crashed in great curls around its base, where dozens of surfers tried their luck on the stampeding white horses. The golden sands of the beach stretched as far as the eye could see. I knew that the spirit of Big Sur lay just a few kilometres to the north, though the magnificent hills and towering cliffs were hidden beyond the horizon. Unless you'd been there, it would be hard to believe what lay beyond this bay, as the coastline here was so mellow in comparison.

In just twenty-four hours I had cycled 150 kilometres that had previously been just a goal, a dream. And now, as I stood at Morro Bay blinking into the distance, it returned to the status of an elaborate dream. The only physical proof I had that I had traversed Big Sur on my bike was my sunburn and a snapshot on my phone of me straddling a red bicycle, wearing my sun-bleached yellow sports bra and salt-stained cycling shorts, smiling ear to ear and throwing my arms up in celebration against vibrant blue skies with Bixby Bridge in the background. Otherwise it was my word against the Earth's.

Breaking my reverie, I kicked off my flip-flops and stepped onto the warm sand and walked towards the water, listening to the rapture of the waves grow louder. At the shoreline the sand was wet and cold, signifying the chill of the ocean. I couldn't wait to dance with those waves. I dropped my clothes to the ground, revealing my bikini and the comical array of tan lines slicing my torso, back, arms, thighs and ankles, and lifted my arms to the sky, ready to run into the ocean.

Just then a lifeguard's truck pulled up beside me. Leaning out of the driver's seat window, his elbow on the door, was a young man, his eyes shaded by aviator sunglasses.

'Are you going swimming?' he asked.

I whipped my head around, startled but trying not to show my surprise. 'Yes – am I allowed?'

On his ski-jump nose, a stripe of white zinc glowed against his otherwise terracotta-tanned and peeling skin. His hair was a mop of blond, his cheeks full and his bright white teeth the perfect straight line. He couldn't have been far into his twenties, though his authoritative demeanour was deceiving.

'Oh, sure, sure,' he said. 'Are you a good swimmer?'

'Yes, I've been swimming all my life,' I replied.

'It's pretty cold in there. You don't have a wetsuit,' he said, stating the obvious.

I wanted to run into the water and leave this inane conversation behind, but something compelled me to engage. 'I know – I love cold water, actually.'

'Well, alright. Just watch out for those rip tides,' he warned.

'I will,' I said. 'My mum always told me, "Never turn your back on the sea." I'll be alright.'

'My name's Tyler, by the way.'

'Hi, Tyler. I'm Jo.'

'Joan?'

'No, it's Jo.'

'Jill?'

'No, Jo. J.O. Jo, as in Joanna. But Jo. Just Jo.' I was getting impatient.

'Wait a second, I detect an accent,' he went on.

Here we go, I thought, then said, 'Yep, I'm actually from London, but I've lived in the States a while now, so my accent is a bit confused.'

'That's cool. I've always wanted to go London and have tea with the Queen. You guys do that, right? Have tea?'

I responded with a small nod then a shake of my head, and tightened my bikini strap, ready to run into the water.

'So, what brings you to these parts?' he continued, trying to keep my attention.

'Actually, I biked here,' I said, feeling quietly proud of myself. 'I'm currently biking the West Coast. I cycled here from Portland. It's kind of a music tour too.'

'Whoa! That's awesome!' He opened his door and stepped out, revealing white socks pulled up to meet his board shorts. Clearly this was not the answer he expected. Nor was what he said next what I was expecting: 'Hey, Jo, take a look at what's in the back of my truck.'

Surprised, I looked where he was pointing but could see nothing. I turned back to him and raised an eyebrow.

Seeing my disdain, he insisted: 'Seriously, go check it out – you won't believe what's in there!'

Reluctantly, I followed his instruction and walked around the back of his truck. He sat in the driver's seat again, watching me through the rear-view mirror.

Lying prostrate, with its legs in the air, a grin on its face and a bright-green sweatband around its neck, was a large dog. It looked so real that for a moment I thought I was staring at something ghoulish – was it a taxidermy pooch? On closer inspection, I realised that it was a large plastic dog from a fairground. It still had the nails in its paws where it had once been attached to the merry-go-round.

I could feel Tyler's eyes burning through me in his rear-view mirror, and a shiver traced down my spine. I walked back to his open door, where his eager green eyes and puppy-dog grin awaited my reaction.

'Well? Did you see it?' he asked excitedly.

'You mean the giant plastic dog? Yeah, hard to miss.'

'Did you read it?' he pushed.

'Read what?' Now I was more confused.

'On his collar. The note. Go back and check it out!' Tyler's voice was rising with giddy enthusiasm.

I picked up my scarf and wrapped it around my waist, then walked back around the truck. On second glance I noticed a ziplock bag attached to the green sweatband. Inside was a piece of paper. I unzipped the bag, pulled out the piece of paper and unfolded it carefully. Its seams were worn and fragile, and scrawled in all capitals was this message:

HI. I'M REX THE TRAVELING DOG, AND I LOVE TO TRAVEL. I HAVE BEEN ACROSS THIS COUNTRY MORE THAN FOUR TIMES OVER. IF YOU ARE ON A JOURNEY THEN I WOULD LOVE TO TRAVEL WITH YOU. BUT, I DON'T LIKE TO BE IN ANY ONE PLACE TOO LONG, SO WHEN YOU REACH YOUR NEXT DESTINATION, GIVE ME TO SOMEBODY ELSE WHO'S ON A JOURNEY.
THANKS. WOOF!

I held the note firmly as the wind tried to whip it from my hand and looked back towards Tyler. He was now standing at the side of his truck. He could see the bemusement in my face and shouted, 'It's a travelling dog! It's Rex the Travelling Dog! Don't you see? You have to take him with you! You guys belong together!'

I looked back at the dog, which now seemed to be staring up at me with a glint in its eye. I patted its head, then picked it up and put it under my arm. Rex's hard plastic body was warm from the sun even though the day had just begun. He was heavier than I had expected, at least 5 kilograms of dead weight.

'I'm not sure I could fit him on my bike,' I told Tyler. 'Besides, I just got rid of a ton of luggage and I don't really want to schlep him around with me.' But as I said this, I felt a combination of guilt, obligation and affection for this inanimate creature. Some part of me wanted to be able to take him with me.

'When do I have to decide?' I asked Tyler. 'I mean, do you have to give him away immediately? I wasn't planning on biking until this afternoon. Can I think about it?' I held Rex out to Tyler.

Tyler smiled, his youthful eyes sparkling conspiratorially. 'Tell you what,' he said, 'why don't you just hang out with Rex for a few hours. Get to know each other. I'll be working on the beach all day. You can let me know what you think when you're ready to leave.'

I agreed and put Rex back under my arm, picked up my towel and the rest of my clothes. Tyler drove back to his post and I walked in the opposite direction to a new spot in the sand where Rex and I could hang out together.

'Guard my things,' I told him, and finally I went for my swim.

I have never made friends with a toy before. At least, not in my adulthood. The only inanimate object that I hold dear is my Eee. Eee is a tiny scrap of blanket. Well, technically two blankets, a pink one and a white one, that, over the last thirty years, have become so completely intertwined that they have formed an inseparable bond. Eee started life as 'Blankee', a nickname for blanket. As a pre-verbal child, however, I couldn't say 'blank' and so I simply said 'Eee'. Eee has been with me ever since. Eee used to be a magnificent blanket that I would drag around with me like Linus van Pelt from *Peanuts*, but over three decades it gradually disintegrated to a pocket-size rag. Eee has been my friend throughout my life, a comfort and also a travel partner. Eee, however, did not come on this bike trip, as I feared that I might lose Eee somehow. Eee was holding the fort at home in Brooklyn, safely tucked away in my closet.

Rex, with his endearingly gormless expression and sun-warmed body, had enough weight that I could lean on him without falling over, and he quickly became a fine beach companion. I lay down in the sand next to him as he happily stared at the ocean. 'Good boy, Rex,' I said, patting his nose.

As I started to doze off, I felt a cool shadow block out the sun. I opened my eyes expecting to see a large cloud in the sky, but instead saw a tall and muscular surfer standing over me. He was staring at Rex, ignoring me completely.

'Wait – is he real?' he asked, water droplets glistening on his bare torso. 'He's not, is he? Is he? Wait – dude!' His accent was quintessentially Californian.

I laughed and sat up. 'No, he's plastic.'

He paused and cocked his head, his handsome face contorting with confusion. 'Oh! I get it. You're, like, protesting, right?' The cogs in his mind were turning almost audibly.

'Protesting? Against what?' Now I was confused.

'This is a dog-free beach. Like, no dogs allowed, dude. Are you, like, protesting about not being allowed to bring your dog to the beach? That's rad.'

At that I laughed so loud the surfer jumped. 'I wish I were the kind of person that would bring a giant fake dog to the beach in protest, but no. I don't even own a real dog. I don't even like dogs that much,' I said, still laughing.

My answer clearly hadn't satisfied his curiosity, so I explained about the note in the ziplock bag, my bicycle journey from Portland, and that Rex and I had only just met and were hanging out on the beach for a while. Eventually he seemed content, and he picked up his surfboard, saluted me goodbye and wandered back towards the waves. I patted Rex on the head and whispered, 'Good boy,' into his plastic ears.

When I returned to the lifeguard tower, Tyler hopped down the steps with a hopeful look on his face. 'Well, are you gonna take him?'

'I'm sorry, I don't think I can. But we had a lovely time together on the beach.'

I handed Rex back to Tyler and kissed his dry nose goodbye. Tyler gave me a hug, Rex awkwardly sandwiched between us.

'Where's your next show?' Tyler asked.

'Oh, it's tomorrow at Linnaea's Cafe in SLO. You should come!'

With that I waved Tyler, and the rest of the lifeguard crew, who were peering nosily through the window at us, au revoir.

21

LINNAEA'S CAFE

I rolled into San Luis Obispo, barely breaking a sweat. The short ride from Morro Bay had been a steady uphill along the highway, but the kilometres had passed almost before I'd had time to notice.

Gliding through the beautiful streets of downtown SLO, I found my way to Linnaea's Cafe. Perched casually on his road bike and chatting to a friend was Greg, my next Warm Showers host. I recognised him by his bike, and by the kind, open expression on his face. I had started to identify the look people who might open their home to travellers like me had.

'Greg?' I said.

'Hey, Jo. You're right on time,' he said in welcome. 'Wanna grab a quick coffee and snack here? Christine is making us dinner.'

After a quick cinnamon roll and tea, we rode to his and his wife's home. The evening was spent in their garden, drinking wine and eating spaghetti. Both he and Christine were semi-professional triathletes, and their garage was filled from floor to ceiling with boxes of Clif Bars and energy gels from companies that sponsored their athletic feats. Christine was training for the Kona Iron Man event, and after dinner she disappeared for a 30-kilometre run, while I took myself to bed.

First thing the next morning I returned to Linnaea's Cafe for breakfast, and to organise things for my show that evening. As soon as I got there, I realised there was a problem: there was no PA system. Remembering that Raff lived not far away in Santa Barbara, and had offered to help if I ever needed it, I decided to get in touch. Sitting in the garden on a small wooden bench next to the fish pond, I texted him: 'Hey Raff, it's Jo. How's everything? So, I wondered if you'd be able to help, after all? Turns out Linnaea's doesn't have any kind of sound system, and I need a PA for my gig tonight! Do you happen to know anyone in SLO who might have one I could borrow?'

Trying not to stare at my phone, I concentrated on my breakfast burrito and iced coffee. Finally, my phone buzzed: 'Hey Jo. Great to hear from you. Totally, you should give my friend Bodhi a call. He should be able to help you. Just tell him you're my friend. So great that you made it to SLO, that's rad!'

I could hear his smiling voice through the letters on the screen. I called the number attached to his message and got through to a voicemail.

'Um, hi, Bodhi, my name's Jo. I'm a friend of Raff and Erisy. Raff told me you might be able to lend me some gear for my show tonight? Give me a call back when you can.' I hesitated. 'Oh, my show is at seven, so I guess sometime before then would be great. Thanks so much.'

I hung up, feeling anxiety rising inside me. I had no idea if I would be able to do my show acoustically.

As I biked back to the house, my phone buzzed in the back of my shorts. I reached back and pulled it out, wiping the sweat from the screen before answering. It was a number I didn't recognise. 'Hello?'

'Hey Jo. It's Bodhi.' The voice on the other end of the line was reminiscent of Jerry Seinfeld, if he'd been a Californian. 'I got your message. I think I can help you out,' he said.

I took a moment, trying to picture his face before responding. 'Thanks so much for calling back at such short notice.'

'For sure, Raff's great. How do you know him, anyway?'
I could hear that he was driving, the crackling wind
breaking the smoothness of his voice.

'I only met him a few days ago,' I replied. 'We were on a
show together in San Francisco.'

'Sweet, that's cool. So I'm just heading home from work,
and I gotta clean up a bit, but why don't you swing by
around five? Does that work for you? You got a car?'

'No, I'm actually travelling by bike. But I'll get a cab –
just send me your address.'

'Bike? Nice,' he said simply, acknowledging what I was
undertaking. 'In that case I'll give you a ride to the venue,
no problem.'

I showered in cool water, my sunburn still stinging from
the last few days of full exposure in Big Sur. At 4.45 p.m.
I called a local taxi number, and ten minutes later I pulled
up outside a large ramshackle abode. In the yard out front
was a work table with a surfboard upturned and a topless
muscular man waxing the bottom of it in the hot sun. The
garage was open, revealing tools, piles of wood, bikes in
various stages of disrepair, surfboards and a motorbike. A
second guy walked out of an unseen door wearing large
goggles, a headband and khaki overalls unbuttoned to his
naval. Neither of them said anything to me, just nodded
and returned to their work.

'Are you Bodhi?' I timidly asked the one with the
surfboard.

'No, I'm Shane,' he said. 'Bodhi should be around here
somewhere.' He continued waxing.

I went to the front door of the house. The door knocker
was adorned with a dead pinecone-wreath tied with a
dusty gold ribbon. Just as I was about to knock, the door
swung open.

'Hey.' I was greeted by curious sea-green eyes and a brilliant smile that glowed through deeply tanned skin. 'I'm Bodhi. How do ya do?' He held out his hand to shake mine, revealing a large tattoo of a twisted oak tree curling around his broad forearm.

I took his hand, unable to find any words.

'Jo, right?' he continued, sensing my befuddlement.

'Yes, hi. I'm Jo. Nice to meet you.' Butterflies congregated in my stomach en masse. I held his green eyes, not wanting my own to drop to his defined bare torso and covering of golden hair, which trailed downward to the shadow of his perfectly formed pelvis muscle – he was wrapped in nothing but a towel. Suddenly aware of my gormless expression, I stepped backward and turned around, looking towards where the taxi had dropped me off.

'Come in,' he said. 'The PA and stuff are in here. Sorry, I was showering. I've been at work all day at the shop. Let me throw on a shirt.'

'No, it's cool. I mean, don't worry about it, I'm easy. Thanks for lending me your gear. Sound gear.' I was a mess.

He beckoned me into the house. His long, golden hair was densely curled and matted from years of ocean swimming, and uneven ringlets bounced on his broad shoulders, giving him the look of Samson. He ducked into a room off the hallway and returned moments later wearing a plaid shirt, unbuttoned.

'Are you a musician too?' I asked.

'Yeah, you could say that. I play the violin and guitar, sing a bit in the shower, ya know.' His tone was modest. 'Here, I hope this works.' He turned on a small speaker and handed me a microphone. 'Try that.'

I sang into the microphone and a clear, pure tone came from the speaker.

'Sweet,' he exclaimed. 'You can use this, then.' We took the whole setup to his car, piling the speaker, microphone and stand into the trunk, trying to find space amid the towels, blankets, toolboxes and wetsuits.

I started to feel a little more relaxed when he offered me a coffee. 'I think there's some on the stove right now,' he said.

We went back into the house. A girl was standing in the kitchen in a miniskirt and tank top, her milky smooth stomach decorated with a bellybutton jewel. She was barefoot and had bright-pink polish on her long toenails that matched her short, pink hair. I felt an irrational pang of jealousy and watched the dynamic between them as Bodhi poured me a cup of coffee. I couldn't figure out what was happening to me. I didn't even know these people, but the energy was as charged as an electric fence. Bodhi and I drank our coffee in strange silence.

'We should probably get going, if that's okay?' I suggested, noticing the time.

As we walked to his car, he whispered conspiratorially, 'That's our new roommate. She's super young. Not quite sure what to make of her yet.'

I could feel his warm breath on my cheek, and the butterflies danced more wildly. I shrugged nonchalantly and said, 'Oh yeah? Cool.'

The front passenger seat was reclined to an almost horizontal position – clearly it was normally used for his surfboard. I tugged at my short dress as it rode up my thighs. Bodhi offered to put the seat up, reaching over me for the lever. Trying to keep my cool, I declined and instead rolled the window down and enjoyed the breeze, which threw my hair into disarray and cooled my blushing cheeks. He put a tape into the player and turned up the volume. Through the crackling old speakers, we listened to a mix tape of 90s grunge music as we rode to Linnaea's Cafe.

I set up on the tiny stage in the back room of the cafe. Bodhi helped me test the sound, and then he sat on the floor, wearing an old leather Indiana Jones–style hat, and quietly waited as the room slowly filled. I'd already sung my first few songs to this room of strangers when I noticed someone with knee socks and board shorts walk in. I looked into the smiling, round-cheeked face: Tyler. I continued singing, and after a little while I heard the clicking of boots. Underneath a velveteen cream Stetson, and wearing a well-pressed denim shirt with a decorative turquoise bolo tie, was Gary, the horse masseur. He smiled and sat down in a chair at the very front.

'Thank you all so much for being here tonight,' I said, 'and for taking a chance on a musician most of you have never heard of before. It's never easy being a touring musician, and I can't tell you how much I appreciate your presence. I'd like to finish this set with one of my newest songs, "Runaway Child".'

I set up my loop pedal and started the song with just a bass line, reminiscent of the doo-wop era. I layered the first voice with a triad above, added a clapping rhythm, then I began the opening lyric: 'I'm a runaway child, Buckle-up shoes and button-down shirt, Oh I want to run wild, I wanna scrape my knees and eat some dirt...'

I looked out to the crowd cheekily, enjoying the realisation that I was now living the lyrics of my song. 'Let go of all this baggage, Be weightless as a butterfly in spring, Or a bird without a cage, Or a perfect diamond without a ring.'

Sweeping my gaze around the room as I sang, I became

aware that we were all runaways in one form or another. Nomads travelling in various directions, searching for answers.

My eyes settled momentarily on Tyler. He smiled at me with a wink, still hopeful about his charm. Bodhi was looking to the floor, listening with his hands clasped on his bent knees as I sang, 'I'm a runaway child, and though I'll go alone I gotta tell you, I can't forget your smile, d'ya wanna come with me, make this a road for two?'

At the end of the show I embraced Gary and Tyler, thanking them for their presence. They had crossed the divide between a one-off encounter and becoming a tangible part of my story and journey. Bodhi broke down the sound system and, once the crowd had dispersed, said to me, 'Where to now, li'l lady?'

'I have to go to a radio interview, actually,' I said. 'Where will you be later?'

'You'll probably find me out on the dance floor at The Library. Some friends are playing there tonight. Have fun on the radio.' He hugged me, patting my back platonically.

I was due to chat during the late-night slot on KCBX radio. I talked to the DJ, Fred, about my bike trip thus far and my upcoming shows. After the interview, Rochelle, Fred's partner, kindly drove me back to the centre of town, where I followed the sound of live music until I found The Library. It was packed with hot, sweating bodies dancing to the riffs of a bluegrass fiddle, banjo and drums. I stood at the door, peering through the heaving dark room, when my hand was grabbed and I was pulled to the middle of the dance floor. Before I had time to think, I was spun around by Bodhi. He was still wearing his leather hat, and his shirt was unbuttoned to the dip beneath his chest bone. I held onto my dress as I laughed in giddy surprise.

Just before midnight, I warned Bodhi that I was going to turn into a pumpkin. Ignoring the voice inside my head, I wished him goodnight, got into a taxi and went home. I was going to be in SLO for another night, and decided I would call him in the morning.

I crept into Greg and Christine's house and lay awake in my quiet room, replaying the surprising events of the day. In the morning I decided to take my bike out to explore the vineyards and beaches, unencumbered by luggage or any particular destination. On my return to the house I passed a road sign: My Way Street. When I got back I called Bodhi, and we arranged to meet that evening.

The fog was rolling in, slowly covering the stars one by one. We lay on a blanket shivering in the cold sand and teasingly egged each other on to go swimming in the black ocean.

'As soon as the fog covers this star,' Bodhi pointed to a faint cluster above our heads, 'then we'll go.'

That was the deal – we would swim only when the fog had covered the stars. We waited and watched but the fog was contrary, building and then evaporating again. It never once reached the stars above our heads.

'Come here, silly.' Bodhi pulled my shivering body into his warm arms. We had been lying side by side with a Victorian seven inches between us for the last hour. His warm fingers entwined with mine as his arms wrapped around my waist. I laid my arm across his stomach, resting my head on his chest.

'There, that's better,' he said, and squeezed me tight.

'Okay, the fog is coming back,' I said, still unable to relax completely. I was like a teenager with a crush, trying in vain to direct our minds back to the prospect of a midnight swim.

Bodhi laughed at my determination to swim tonight. I looked up at him and kissed him. I wanted to stop his laughter, feign seriousness, but I hadn't intended to kiss him already. My body-mind was taking over and I was surprised at my forwardness. He kissed me back, and for a moment it was as though the waves were put on pause. Just as quickly the world sped into fast-forward again, and in unison we stood up and ran towards the ocean, throwing our clothes off, two naked silhouettes running into the glowing black ocean.

'Stay with me tonight,' he insisted as he drove me back to Greg and Christine's.

'I can't,' I said. 'I have to get up early and bike to Buellton tomorrow. It's a long ride and I want to get a good sleep.' I was confused by my own coyness. I was scared of something. He didn't insist further.

As I got out of the car, I leaned over and kissed him. 'Come to Buellton tomorrow. Stay with me there.'

22

BIRD'S EYE VIEW

SAN LUIS OBISPO – BUELLTON – SANTA BARBARA:
187 KILOMETRES

I left Greg and Christine's home with a newly acquired rubber chicken strapped to the top of my ukulele case. When I'd told Greg about Rex the Travelling Dog, he'd gone rummaging in the garage and dug out this odd thing. Inscribed on its yellow belly were the names of two cities and two dates.

'This chicken was actually a wedding present,' Greg told me. 'It was given to us by some good friends who had acquired it as their wedding present, with the premise that it should continue to travel and be passed on to others going through life-changing events – such as biking the West Coast. I think you should have it now.' He handed me the rubber chicken almost ceremoniously, and then we waved goodbye.

With every bump I heard the friendly squeak of the

chicken from one of my rear panniers. It added some comic relief to what was otherwise a rather dull journey from San Luis Obispo to Buellton. I followed the cycle path, which mostly avoided the highway, leading me instead through monotonous strip malls and residential streets. For a while I was stuck behind a pickup truck that was spewing out thick fumes; it had a red, white and blue 'Vote Trump' poster on it. I wanted to get through this particular suburb as quickly as I could.

I also needed to eat, as my own engines were winding down fast. In the sleepy town of Los Alamos I came across an artisanal bakery that served nitro-brewed coffee and handsome handmade cakes. I had hit the jackpot. Sitting underneath an oversize parasol, I let the sugar and caffeine flow into my bloodstream as I relaxed in the shade, eyes closed and a smile on my lips. I was only 30 kilometres short of Buellton.

The yellow hills rolled liltingly alongside the highway, burnt grass thirsty for rain that would never come. The shoulder was wide and I enjoyed a long stretch of downhill. I free-wheeled, conserving my energy, and smiled each time I hit a stone or a bump as the rubber chicken squeaked behind me. Small, scrubby trees were scattered along the edge of the road, their tiny but dense leaves providing cooling shade for the animals that sheltered beneath. The azure sky throbbed in the blistering heat. There was no breeze. Aside from the passing cars and my own body, everything was still.

Then, like a gunshot resounding at the start of a race, a few hundred sparrows sprang from their hiding place amid the tiny leaves of the tiny trees, displacing the air with a sudden shock. They soared upward and performed a ballet of murmurations, slicing the sky into a thousand

tiny pieces, rising and falling like ash cascading from a
burning building. I was transfixed, and through my dry
lips and smiling eyes I began to whisper words that would
become a new song:

> *Ballet of birds in the sky exploded out of a treetop*
> *On the side of the road,*
> *Casting their net, catching dreams*
> *Of every last sleeper on his way to being free.*
> *Silently we sing to each other*
> *Like two lovers on the wing,*
> *Breathlessly we inhale every colour,*
> *As far as the eye can see,*
> *A ballet of birds.*
> *Drifting along not a cloud*
> *To answer any shadow's mischievous ways,*
> *A lacework of song against the blue,*
> *They rise and they fall*
> *Like the breaking of a wave.*
> *And they dance like a thousand kisses*
> *Caught in a tornado's spin,*
> *Feathered hands caressing the spaces*
> *We are crowded in,*
> *This romance with loneliness*
> *Survives on the tales of the wind,*
> *Beating fast invisible hearts ever changing,*
> *A ballet of birds.*

A few kilometres outside of Buellton I saw its welcome
sign. A cartoon of an overweight chef loomed above me

on a giant billboard: wielding a mallet above his white hat, he was ready to pound down onto a nail held above a tiny pea by his beanpole-thin underdog and into the bubbling pot of lumpy brown soup. In giant red brush-script were the words 'Buellton, Everything for the Traveler', and beneath, 'Pea Anderson Inn, World Famous Split Pea Soup'. I had booked a room at the Pea Anderson Inn, but had not connected the name with the old-fashioned and detestable food item. I stopped beneath the billboard as my odometer clocked 1000 miles, or over 1600 kilometres. Leaning my bike against the wooden structure, the rubber chicken squeaking as I did so, I quietly celebrated this milestone with a bite of protein bar washed down with warm water.

The only clue that I had arrived in Buellton itself was a gas station, a budget motel and a sign pointing towards the Pea Anderson Inn. 'I guess this is it,' I said to myself, and reached back to squeak the chicken by way of a response. I checked in at the motel. It was 5 p.m.

I had told Bodhi to come at around 5.30, but had not heard from him all day and wondered if he would turn up after all. I was exhausted. The miles from San Luis Obispo had been arduous, boring and mostly uphill, but for the final stretch. I scrubbed the sweat and road grime off my skin with the washcloth and the small bar of soap provided by the hotel. I shaved my legs with a single-blade razor and cut my knee. Blood pooled in a neat circle around my feet as I rinsed my hair. Stepping out of the small shower cubicle, I dried off and attempted to stop the bleeding with a square of toilet paper. I was nervous, and my blood-sugar levels were low.

I hadn't quite pulled my tank top over my head when I heard a knock at the door. I looked in the mirror. My hair was still dripping, the tissue stuck to my knee had soaked red, and my top was inside out. 'Just a minute,' I called.

Sunlight crept in the gap under the door, punctuated by the shadows of two feet standing close to the other side. I couldn't help but smile. I threw the tissue into the trash, left my shirt as it was and squeezed my sopping wet hair in my hands, creating a wet spot on my right breast. I gave up and opened the door. Silhouetted by the sun, wearing leather boots, jeans and a brown leather jacket, Bodhi looked like a sepia snapshot from a spaghetti western.

'Hi,' he said quietly, his green eyes smiling.

'Hi,' I replied, mirroring his smile. 'Come in.'

He stepped towards me and pulled me into his arms. I could feel his heart beating through his chest onto mine. He was as nervous as I was. He kissed my face and I turned my lips towards his. With the curtains open and the sounds of other residents swimming in the pool two floors below, we let the universe spin around us until dawn, when we would have to say goodbye.

In the morning we walked through the no man's land that was Buellton to find some strong coffee. We held hands tightly, though we barely said a word. Breaking the silence, a man driving a grey Prius called out of his window, 'I'd fuck her!'

We said goodbye in the parking lot of the Pea Anderson Inn. My bicycle pointed south, Bodhi's motorbike to the north. I was in my lycra shorts, Bodhi in his jeans; I in cycling shoes, he in leather boots; my helmet strapped on, his waiting upon his handlebars. We kissed once more, then our lips parted with the irreversibility of a butterfly leaving its cocoon.

I pushed my bike towards the traffic lights, then stopped and turned. Bodhi already had his back to me as he donned his leather jacket and helmet. He didn't see me looking at him as I second-guessed my direction, the idea of travelling north with him flashing across my eyes. Then the light turned green and, like the migratory bird I had become, I pushed southward. I never did hear the sound of his engine as it bled into the sea of traffic.

I began to understand how author and traveller Laurie Lee might have been feeling when he wrote: 'It is easier to leave than to stay behind and love.'

'Just leaving Buellton!' I shouted above the roar of the highway into my voice recorder, 'I don't quite know what just happened, but…I just had the most amazing time and… now I'm leaving, and I don't know quite why, and…' I was fumbling for words as though trying to describe a dream.

I felt compelled to detail all my memories of Pea Anderson Inn before they faded, like everything to beyond the horizon seemed to. As I raced down Highway 1, I shouted into my phone, questioning what could be forcing me forward when I might have found what I'd been looking for all along, and in Buellton of all places. I continued blaring out intimate details, sure that nobody would hear me, when suddenly a voice made me leap from my skin.

'Where are you headed?'

I almost jumped out of my saddle, trying to catch my heart as it lurched to my throat at the sound of this phantom voice. Skipping along on my tail was a silver-haired, narrow-faced road cyclist, his eyes hidden behind razor-blade shades, his sinewy thighs powering his fibreglass bike with the speed and ease of a gazelle.

'Sorry, I didn't mean to frighten you,' he shouted. He was coat hanger thin, a Sunday morning cyclist pounding out as many miles as he could before noon.

'No, it's okay,' I called back, embarrassed. 'I, erm, was just talking to myself.' I focused on the road ahead.

'You must have travelled a ways with that setup,' he said, pointing to my two remaining panniers.

'Yes – from Portland, actually. I used to have a lot more gear with me. But I'm almost done. I'm heading to Los Angeles.'

'You're going all the way to LA today?' He looked impressed. 'That's a long stretch.'

'No, no, just to Santa Barbara.'

'That's where I'm going. We can ride together, if you like,' he offered. 'There's quite a sharp corner up ahead, just before Gaviota Beach. Take it easy and watch out for the cars.' He pointed to the steeply sweeping road ahead, which was thick with rushing traffic, and took the lead.

I barrelled down the hill behind him, my thoughts dissipating in a flurry of gravity and wind. In an exhilarating moment I passed the treacherous corner and saw him signalling for me to pull over up ahead. He had a seriousness about him, a grandfatherly air that I trusted. I signalled right and swooped into the rest stop.

'My name's Mark.' Still wearing his helmet, his sunglasses now tucked into the neck of his jersey, he held out his gloved hand in greeting.

'Mark, it's nice to meet you. I'm Jo.'

'Hungry? Here, take this,' he said, and handed me an open bag of fig cookies.

'Thanks so much. These were my favourite after-school snacks when I was a kid.' Noticing the larger chunks of fresh fig and gooey molasses between the oats, I asked, 'Did you make these?'

'Of course. I never eat those processed bars anymore. Do you know what's in them? I want to be in charge of everything I put in my body,' he told me proudly.

I didn't want to admit I'd been surviving on protein bars all month, so instead told him the fig cookies were delicious.

He offered me another. 'So you're biking the West Coast, eh? Are you alone?'

'Yes – well, since Arcata, anyway. I had a friend with me for the first week.'

'That's very brave of you. I've always wanted to bike the whole coast, but I used up my adventure days when I was much younger.'

'Wait, you live here but you've never biked the whole coast? You must,' I remarked.

Mark looked at me, his blue eyes twinkling, his cheeks creasing into a concertina of kind wrinkles. 'When I was eighteen I travelled the world on my own,' he said. 'I was in New Zealand hitchhiking my way across the country. I had been walking along the highway and not one car had passed all day. I was hungry, tired and, I'll admit, a bit concerned. Then I heard the roar of a plane engine overhead, then all of a sudden the plane was right in front of me – it landed on the highway. It gave me the fright of my life.' He laughed, then continued. 'I stood completely frozen. I thought I'd lost my mind. The pilot climbed out of the cabin and walked towards me, wearing those old-fashioned pilot goggles. You know the ones?'

I nodded, listening intently still chewing on the fig cookies.

'The pilot asked where I was going. Wellington, I told him, and without skipping a beat he replied, "Me too – hop in." Before I knew it I was flying across the mountains in a light plane and was in Wellington within the hour. That was a highlight of my adventures, to say the least!' He laughed louder this time, shaking his head.

'That's incredible,' I said, my eyes like dinner plates.

'Anyway, that's all to say that I know a little how you must be feeling right now, on this big adventure, all alone. Hey, I just had an idea. These days I actually own and fly helicopters. I would be happy, and honoured, to return the favour of that pilot and give you a flight around Santa Barbara this evening – if you're not busy, of course.'

In his piercing blue eyes I could see the young man hitchhiking through New Zealand.

'I'm sorry, say that again?' I wasn't sure I had heard him right.

Raising his voice to be heard over the waterfall of traffic, he repeated, slowly and surely, 'Would you like a helicopter ride this evening? My gift, from one traveller to another.'

Santa Barbara was just 150 kilometres from my destination, Santa Monica Pier, and Erisy had invited me to stay with her before I set out on this final leg. I was excited to see her again, to close the gap between our initial encounter in San Francisco and draw our friendship into the present again. I had told her that I'd be arriving at her house at about five o'clock, but I was on track to be a couple of hours early.

I was used to riding at an average of 15 to 20 kilometres per hour, depending on the terrain and the wind. I had found that was the perfect pace, allowing me to enjoy the views and not kill myself with sheer effort. But Mark, unladen and on a bike that weighed less a quarter of mine, had kept our pace at an unrelenting 25 kilometres per hour. The road was flat and the tailwind consistent, and I'd embraced the challenge of keeping up with him, even with my loaded panniers and heavier touring bike. However, biking at this speed had one major drawback: I'd had to sacrifice the pleasure of taking in the details of the ride. We were on a mission to get to Santa Barbara as fast as possible. Mark was tracking his heart rate, speed, calories and every other measurement that he could log and compare with those of his cycling buddies later. All I wanted to log was the incredible sight of the Pacific Ocean beyond the eucalyptus trees.

At a quarter to three I knocked on Erisy's door. She opened it with a beaming smile.

'Erisy, you're not going to believe this,' I said. 'We're going for a helicopter ride this evening!'

She threw her arms around me and squealed in delight.

From the air, sunset over Santa Barbara County was like gazing into the heart of an opal. Mark flew us in his helicopter, which lifted vertically off the ground like the bubbles in the Great Glass Elevator, drawing us up into the pearlescent blue sky.

We soared south, flying over Oprah Winfrey's estate, watching for dolphins cutting through the rippling ocean, and chasing the giant ball of fire as it dipped beneath the yellow horizon. As we turned and pointed north once more, the sight of the coastline disappearing into the distance took my breath away. I pictured the road trailing northward, rewinding through Buellton, over Big Sur, through Carmel. Lonely footprints tracing backwards across the cold sands on Half Moon Bay, the Golden Gate Bridge bowing with its many voyagers, Mill Valley, Mendocino; where was the couple with the bacon sandwiches now? Further north still were the effervescent Avenue of the Giants, Pepperwood, Steve and his red Volvo, Arcata, the woman in the wheelchair, Eugene, Salem and Portland.

A road turning and weaving through a thousand eyelets, now threaded with an experience that would forever link and join the terrain with the beating of an eager heart. I knew in that moment that the Pacific Coast Highway would never look the same to me again. It throbbed with memory, bulged with life. In my mind I saw its fingers stretch open, palm faced upward, offering answers to questions I would never have asked had I not traversed its unforgiving and ever-giving road on two wheels.

Mark, Erisy and I, three near strangers in an aluminium bubble soaring high above the Pacific with the freedom and grace of eagles, celebrated all of this in the most unexpected of ways.

23

YOUR MIND IS PLAYING
A TRICK ON YOU

SANTA BARBARA – VENTURA: 53 KILOMETRES

I delayed my departure from Erisy's house the following day. Now that the end was so close, I didn't want to pull the drawstrings shut on this journey. Time wasn't going to wait for me, but I could at least imagine that I could stave it off by staying still for a little while longer. I decided I would take my time and cycle this last leg slowly, mindfully.

I had the email address of a woman named Rachel, who, I had been told, would likely be able to put me up for the night in Ventura. She responded quickly with a short note – 'Yes. What time will you arrive?' – and her address.

I waved Erisy goodbye in the late afternoon and took the bike path out of Santa Barbara, riding with the sunset to my right. The intensity of the Pacific Ocean had changed as I travelled south, turning from the black-grey of the Oregon coastline to the warm, purple-blue of Southern California.

It was a 50-kilometre ride from Santa Barbara to Ventura. My Ortlieb panniers now all but completely empty, and the road ahead all but completely straight, I barely noticed the miles pass beneath my wheels. Meditating only on the horizon, I imagined that I could see Santa Monica beyond the winding cliffs to the south-east. As the sun set to the west, my shadow stood tall against the golden hills to my left, and I stared at it like Peter Pan as it followed my every move.

Late-summer dolphins performed their twilight ballet, punctuating each translucent wave. Backlit by the setting sun, the scene was like a holy monument, a rippling of stained glass in a vast church. Mesmerised, my shadow and I slowed to a halt and stopped to worship the Pacific and this revelation of life, until the sun was just a sliver of fire on the cobalt horizon.

As dusk settled in like dust on an abandoned house, I arrived in Ventura. The first direction I'd had to follow all day was: 'In six hundred feet, turn left on Olive Street.' I came to a small cottage surrounded by sunflowers and tomato plants. I pushed open the low metal gate and wheeled my bike along the narrow brick path towards a colourfully painted garage at the back of the garden. Bent over a workbench, wrench in hand, was Rachel. She was wearing denim overalls and red Birkenstock sandals, and her strawberry-blond hair was tied up on top of her head. A paint-splattered transistor radio sat on the shelf above her head, the coat hanger antenna stuck on with gaffer tape. She didn't hear me approach over the crackling voice of the news reporter.

'Hi, Rachel?' I cleared my throat and said again, this time louder, 'Rachel? Hi. Sorry I'm late.' She looked up, her hair whipping back from her forehead.

'Oh, great, you're here. I wasn't worried. I have to go to a meeting now, though, so I can't entertain you. There are sheets and a towel inside for you – make yourself at home. Actually, hold on,' she said in rapid fire, then turned the radio off. 'Here, you can put your bike there. I won't be home too late, but I do have to leave early in the morning, so if I don't see you before you go to sleep, or wake up for that matter, have a great journey onward.' She wiped her hands on her overalls and pulled down the garage door, closing it with a metallic bang. 'In the morning just lift this latch – but be careful, the door is really heavy. It'll spring up if you don't hold onto it.'

She led me through the back door and into the kitchen. 'I'm afraid I don't have any food to offer you except a hard-boiled egg and some crackers.' She handed me a pile of sheets and a towel. 'Excuse me, I have to change for my meeting.' She disappeared into her bedroom.

I stood in the small kitchen, aware of my cleats clicking upon the tile floor. Holding my clean sheets, I admired the colourful clay tiles above the sink and Aga oven. Under a fruit-fly cage on a wooden table in the middle of the room was a small pile of crackers and a boiled egg. I decided I would come to that later.

Rachel re-emerged, dressed in a smart grey jacket and clean linen trousers. 'Okay, gotta run,' she said. 'Take care now. Oh, and when you leave tomorrow, please lock the door and hide the key beneath the tomato plant outside.' She gave me a quick hug, the scent of rose perfume rising from her wrist, then left me alone in her home.

Quiet surrounded me. The furniture sat still, neatly tucked away. The lace trim on the small window above the deep porcelain sink seemed to sigh. Two antique wooden chairs sat lonely under the table. In the living room, deep-green throw cushions had been placed purposefully in the nooks of the couch. Oil paintings, textured and reaching from the canvas, framed in unvarnished wood and depicting seascapes, hung on the wall. Abstract wooden sculptures, some as tall as me, stood on the floor, and above them, on hooks, hung a selection of instruments. Mandolins, banjos, guitars, violins, some with missing strings, others that looked well-loved and often used.

Monopolising the small bathroom was a lion's foot tub, enclosed by a floral shower curtain. Above the sink, a pattern of blue mosaic tiles surrounded a small mirror that reflected a face I was slowly getting to know. I made my nest on the sofa bed, and then washed away the miles, the sunblock and salt in the deep tub. Then I repacked my panniers for the last time. I had gone to sleep before Rachel returned home, and when I awoke in the morning, the house was empty again.

Sixth of September, 6 a.m. I woke without an alarm, my body clock now keenly tuned in to the dawn. Tightly curled up in a blue-and-green tartan wool blanket, lying on the thin sofa-bed mattress, I gazed into the half-light, fully rested, yet heavy with the knowledge that today would be my last day on the road. My panniers lay at the end of the couch, my cycling clothes neatly folded on top, ready to slip on. I had planned to have an early start and take my time getting to Los Angeles, but now I lay in perfect stillness, my arms cinched against my sides. The time-stopping bliss of sleep had been shattered by the dawn, and by my awareness that the inevitable finish line was now but a matter of time away.

A month ago, I had envisioned that this day would be one of relief and excitement, ignited by joyful impatience to put down my bike and strip my behind of padded lycra once and for all. I never anticipated the whirlpool of doubt and sadness in which I swirled now. Heat stung the back of my eyes, and a tear glided down each cheek as I stared unblinkingly at the ceiling.

Through dilated pupils I sank back into my memory, and watched as the faces and places I had encountered over the last five weeks drifted before my mind's eye like distant clouds. I smiled in my reverie, and my arms found their way out of the blankets, which I threw to the side of the sofa bed, revealing my deeply tanned legs. Limb by limb, I brought myself up to sitting.

Silence surrounded me, but for a thin, salty breeze that whispered in through the window behind the sofa. I planted my feet firmly on the worn rug and stood, letting out a sigh, wiping the tears from my face. 'Shit, Jo. How did this day already arrive?'

The painting of a wild ocean, frozen in its frame, seemed to answer me: *Time plus motion, time plus motion.*

I pulled on my lycra shorts and sports bra. I had saved a clean and unused set of clothes in the bottom of my bag for this day – a special uniform for the final sprint. Half-dressed and hungry, I padded from room to room, re-examining the strange sculptures that decorated the floor, now so different in the dawn light. I looked in the small mirror as I brushed my teeth, my mind dwelling on what lay ahead. This evening I would be in Los Angeles.

As I roamed from the bathroom to the living room and the kitchen, I noticed yellow post-it notes stuck to the walls. Looking closer, I saw that each was inscribed with a message, a quote, a mantra. Just above the stove, on the same tiles I had admired the night before, were two post-it notes stuck together. *Were these there last night?* I wondered as I leaned in to read them.

In neat handwriting were the words: *Your mind is playing a trick on you and making you think that something in the future is more important than this moment.*

I took the hint. It was time to get my shit together and hit the road for one last time.

24

FINAL FLIGHT

VENTURA – SANTA MONICA: 90 KILOMETRES

Carefully lifting the brightly painted garage door, I retrieved my trusty steed. I bade my bike a good morning, as one would any companion. With my hand on her handlebars, we walked back down the brick path, past the tomato plants, under which I left the key, and back through the small gate.

The early-morning air was crisp and clear on my eyes, and the scent of the ocean sweet upon my tongue. My wheels passed almost silently over the cool tarmac and I felt, once again, at home. Rounding the corner from Olive Street to Main, I could sense an impatience about the morning traffic. Pale and tired faces sat behind wound-up windows. Summer was over for everybody but me. Two children dressed in dark jackets, with large backpacks slung over their shoulders, walked lazily towards a school bus.

I wove through downtown Ventura, towards the pier

that marked the edge of town. The sun rose slowly and with steady purpose, casting a soft golden light over the oil-blue ocean. Out on the silken water, cutting amphibious silhouettes into the gentle waves, a dozen surfers bobbed balletically on their boards, their glistening backs waiting patiently for a surge big enough to ride. Everything was in relief, the world a series of negatives in a darkroom. Each pedal stroke felt important and loaded with meaning, each rotation bringing me closer to my journey's end.

I left Ventura via the winding bike path that hugged the coastline. Sand crunched beneath my tires. Greedy seagulls picked at trash that had been left overnight. A woman slept on a bench outside a public toilet, wrapped up in bundles of clothing pulled up to her chin, her long and matted hair draped over the armrest. A few yards further on I passed a young man with a blanket slung over his bony shoulders; he acknowledged me with a slow, scanning gaze. Just as the bike path ended, I passed a third wanderer, a barefoot man pushing a shopping cart filled with plastic bags and blankets. His hair was dreadlocked around his neck, his stubble white against his dark, leathery skin, which hung slack over his sharp cheekbones. His eyes shone out from deep sockets as blue as the ocean beside us, and under the California sun we wished each other good morning. His face lit up with a childlike charm as we made this fleeting connection before continuing on our solitary journeys.

The road was flat, the wind soft. The distance seemed to evaporate; every time I looked at my odometer, another 15 kilometres had passed. I wanted to pedal backwards, rewind, reverse, retreat, but now I was on a fast-forward track and there was no turning around. By 9 a.m. the sun was a white ball in the sky. I had been riding on an empty bike path since just after dawn, and now I was approaching the highway again.

At the fork ahead was a large green road sign and, in oversized white letters, with an arrow pointing to the right, words I had thought I would never see: 'Santa Monica'.

I paused. Alone on the road, I felt the wind fall from my sails. *If only,* I thought, *I could turn around and ride back north.* The end, the end, the end. I didn't want this to end. But, as if my legs belonged to someone else, my pedals turned and I continued south. The vibration of the cars thundering through my wheels, the sound of the wind in my ears and the endless sky above sent an ecstatic thrill through me. I felt powerful and free.

The Pacific Coast Highway had become my greatest friend and mentor, revealing secrets about life that I could never have found anywhere else. Accepting my destiny for this day, I pushed down hard on the pedals and built up my speed in celebration of the road ahead. My legs burned and my lungs expanded like the outstretched wings of an eagle, my senses heightening as I travelled side-by-side with the speeding giants. I felt a blissful vulnerability, and perhaps a foolish trust that I was safe here. I had learnt to embrace the black-and-white options of life on a bicycle. It was always do or die, and I felt simultaneously invisible and larger than life. On the road I was home.

By 10 a.m. I was hungry. Ventura was 50 kilometres behind me, just another memory. At the bottom of a sweeping hill was a beach campsite. I let my brakes go and sped towards an early lunch break. My remaining two panniers contained nothing but a few items of clothing and some food. In San Luis Obispo I had sent everything else to Los Angeles, leaving me with maybe 10 kilograms to carry instead of the forty I had started with in Portland. From a paper grocery bag in the right pannier I pulled out a bagel, an avocado and a packet of sliced Swiss cheese. My last supper on the road.

I sat on a dilapidated sandy bench, my steed propped up beside me, her wheels rim deep in silken sand. I savoured each mouthful of stale bagel and warm cheese, peacefully staring out at the turquoise Pacific as it lapped at the dirty white shoreline.

I hadn't wanted to rush this final day, but the kilometres continued to disappear. The only way to stop them was to stop riding, but that was not an option. I flowed along with the warm current, south, south, south.

Perched high above the ocean, I came to another road sign. Upon a swirl of blue and green were shining white letters that spelled out: 'Malibu, 27 Miles of Scenic Beauty'. The landscape had been gradually changing from rugged to refined, and elaborate houses started to appear, clinging to the cliffs like giant molluscs. I had ridden into the heart of California Dreaming.

After days of silence, the sound of the ocean and tyre-on-tarmac my only companion, I decided I needed a soundtrack to accompany this cinematic moment. I chose the Beach Boys' compilation album *Perfect Harmony*, and turned the volume up as loud as my iPhone speakers could manage. A cappella harmonies singing 'The Warmth of the Sun' bloomed through the space around me. The Beach Boys and I rolled into Malibu with the sun in our eyes and the wind at our backs.

Rising and falling with the road, next to the water one

moment and high above the next, the sun was hot and the blue of the midday Pacific was calling to me. The tide was high along the private beaches of Malibu Road, leaving barely any sand visible. I pushed my bike through a white gate between two futuristic stilt-houses above the wild water. Hooking my handlebars over the railing to stop my bike from tumbling down the steep concrete steps that led to the beach below, I carefully stepped down towards the water.

Waves swirled around a large rock and crashed down heavily, sending up great sprays of white foam. I stood for a few minutes watching the water, calculating its strength against my own. Beneath the open foundations of one of the houses I changed, struggling out of my sweat-soaked lycra and into my bikini. I left my clothes tucked under a rock. I walked cautiously into the foaming water, my tired legs thankful as the cold rushed around my hot muscles. The drag of the current was strong and unpredictable, tugging at my legs. I could hear the distant Sirens calling me to their sorry embrace.

I didn't go in beyond my waist, instead I sat down on the sand and dug my feet in as an anchor, and let the waves wash over my head with an ever-changing rhythm. With the salt of the Pacific on my sunburnt skin, and the dazzling reflection of the California skies in my squinting eyes, I returned to my bike.

'Watch out, little lady, the hill up ahead is pretty darn steep,' two fat old men called out from a roadside bench as I approached Point Dume.

They didn't know where I had come from; how could they know all I had been through? From their viewpoint, I was just a woman riding her bike with a smile on her face. They couldn't know how strong I was, or how many hills I had conquered, devoured, enjoyed, befriended.

'I can't wait!' I called back, and rode on before they could answer.

The smog unfurled in a purple haze over the city of Los Angeles. Tall buildings reached up as if from the ocean floor, pushing past the kelp forests, breaking through the earth in a metamorphosis from nature to the industrial revolution.

Then, like a mirage, I saw it: the circular outline of the Ferris wheel and the snaking frame of the roller-coaster, recognisable only as the Santa Monica Pier. I fixed my eyes on this symbol of summertime fun and pedalled on, listening to my breath and trying not to stop. Breathe, pedal, breathe. I had taught myself to carry on no matter what. Breath, pedal, breathe.

The pier grew clearer, the roller-coaster bigger. I could almost see the people sitting in the Ferris wheel's carriages, hear the sound of cheerful voices screaming above the rush of traffic and the crash of waves. A sign with a picture of a bicycle and an arrow to the right led me off the highway for the last time, and with a light crunch my wheels met a submerged cycle path.

Unused volleyball nets lined up along the yellow sand like soldiers awaiting orders. Beach cruisers with handlebars up to their riders' ears rolled by me. Shirtless backs and sun-bleached hair, tanned skin crinkled like aged leather and shining with sweat, joggers, walkers, bikers, poodles, children, men and women, young and old – they all oozed past me like a vintage movie backdrop. After miles and miles of open road, I was thrown onto this walkway crowded with day trippers, and I felt more alone than I had since the seclusion of Benbow Drive. I had travelled almost 2000 kilometres to reach this friendly bike path, and in the heat of the midday sun I could see each of those kilometres evaporating as if they never were. The countless hills, the pain, the triumphs would all reach their completion on this path of least resistance.

I took off my helmet, my bike cap and my sunglasses, and rode the final couple of kilometres with the wind blowing through my sea-salty hair. I barely turned the pedals, the momentum of the end enough to pull me forward. The pier grew larger as I got nearer, and the smell of candy corn permeated the hot air. I could hear kids shouting with joy, muffled music across the breeze. No one seemed to notice me. I was on a path of inevitability. I was going to arrive and, one way or another, my journey was going to come to an end.

Then it happened. No drama, no witnesses. I stopped riding, stepped off my bike and looked up at the Santa Monica Pier, right above me. Looking down again, I saw 1154 miles on my odometer – 1857 kilometres. Then the world blurred with tears. I looked around but there was nobody to tell, nobody to hug, nobody to confirm that I had done it. My tears were not tears of sadness but of gratitude – for this life, and for the gifts it had given me this past month. They were also tears of mourning, for a life I had now left behind. I knew in this moment that nothing was going to be the same.

I was never more alone than in this moment, surrounded by crowds of people enjoying a beautiful September day on the beach. Maybe I was invisible after all. I asked a smiling couple if they'd take a photo of me standing with my bike, my rubber chicken and the pier. They were salty and sunburned just like me. I thanked them and watched as they walked towards the water, hand in hand.

I tried to fight the feelings rising in me and closed my eyes, mentally projecting myself to a different place. But there was nowhere else I could go, and nowhere else I would rather be. I was here, and that alone was perfect.

GEAR LIST

ORTLIEB BAGS
2 rear pannier bags (yellow)
2 front pannier bags (yellow)
1 handlebar bag (yellow)
6 dry bags (multiple colours)
1 saddlebag
1 Safe-It waterproof phone case

WATER BOTTLES
CamelBak 3-litre water reservoir
3 bike store own-brand water bottles

RACKS
Back: Tubus Tara
Front: Tubus Tara

PUMP
Vibrelli mini bike pump
1 puncture repair kit (though I never needed it!)

BIKE
Condor Cycles Heritage steel-framed touring bike
(racing red)

SHOES
Specialized women's Riata mountain bike shoes (brown)

HELMET
Giro Atmos (blue/black)

CLOTHING
2 pairs of basic women's cycling shorts
4 pairs of sport socks
2 sports bras
1 merino wool jersey
1 windbreaker
1 night-vision jersey
1 pair of leggings
2 tank tops
6 pairs of underwear

PEDALS
Shimano PD-M520

SADDLE
Specialized Women's Lithia Comp Gel

UKULELE AND CASE
Mitchell Concert Ukulele
No-name brand, super cheap, hard case

LOOP PEDAL
RC-Boss 30

THE GREAT SONG CYCLE TOUR DATES

2 August	House Concert, Portland
6 August	Eugene Farmers Market / Axe and Fiddle, Cottage Grove
12 August	The Sanctuary Art House, Arcata
17 August	Kala Brand Ukulele, Petaluma
19 August	Octopus Literary Library, Oakland
20 August	Red Poppy Art House, San Francisco
23 August	Sofar Sounds at Hyde Street Studios, San Francisco
25 August	Santa Cruz Coffee Roasting Co. Santa Cruz / Zizzo's Wine Bar, Capitola
26 August	Santa Cruz Coffee Roasting Co. Aptos
28 August	UUCMP Church, Carmel
1 September	Linnaea's Cafe, San Luis Obispo / KCBX Radio Interview, SLO
2 September	The Porch Cafe, Santa Margarita
8 September	ASCAP Headquarters, Los Angeles

ACKNOWLEDGEMENTS

I'd like to thank the following for their direct and indirect contributions to this journey and book: My parents, Libby and Raphael, for their tireless (no pun intended!) love, and my entire family for filling my life with music. Haggai Cohen-Milo, for encouraging me to follow through with the idea in the first place. Daniel, my beloved partner in life, who has heard this story countless times and still listens. Ortlieb USA, for sponsoring me with gear. Kala Brand Music Co., for gifting me two beautiful ukuleles. The Banff Centre for Arts and Creativity, for giving me space to write. Condor Cycles, for making beautiful bicycles. *Boreas*, for being always at my back. Last but by no means least, I thank every person I mention in this book – for your shelter, laughter, support, food, friendship and encouragement; although most names have been altered, my gratitude abounds nonetheless.

ABOUT THE AUTHOR

Joanna Wallfisch is a critically acclaimed singer-songwriter and multi-instrumentalist, whose musical style combines her classical roots with her love of jazz, art-song, folk and poetry of all kinds. Born and raised in London, she studied jazz performance at the Guildhall School of Music & Drama. In 2012 she moved to New York City, where she performed and collaborated with musicians such as Wynton Marsalis, Kenny Werner, Sam Newsome, Lee Konitz and Dan Tepfer. She is an active member of WIJO (Women In Jazz Organization).

Joanna has released five albums of original music: *Wild Swan* (2011), *The Origin of Adjustable Things* (2015, Sunnyside Records), *Gardens In My Mind* (2016, Sunnyside Records), *Blood & Bone* (2018, Sea Gardens Publishing) and *Far Away From Any Place Called Home* (2019, Sea Gardens Publishing). Her songs and vocals have also been featured on movies and commercials.

As well as performing internationally, Joanna is a passionate educator and takes her songwriting and teaching skills to outreach programs, schools and colleges. In 2016 she travelled to Mumbai with Songbound, an outreach initiative that brings the transformative power of music to some of India's poorest and most marginalised children. She has also worked in Los Angeles with non-profit organisation Urban Voices Project (UVP), bringing music education and choir to the Skid Row community. With UVP Joanna co-leads Family Sing, a music program for children and mothers experiencing homelessness.

For more on Joanna, and to view her touring schedule, visit www.joannawallfisch.com.